CONVERSION
and the
CATECHUMENATE

CONVERSION
and the
CATECHUMENATE

edited by
Robert D. Duggan

paulist press ✒ *new york/ramsey*

Library of Congress
Catalog Card Number: 83-62949

ISBN: 0-8091-2614-1

Published by Paulist Press
545 Island Road, Ramsey, N.J. 07446

Printed and bound in the
United States of America

Contents

Introduction

This book is meant for all those whose lives and ministries have been touched by that mysterious divine-human encounter we try to name with the word "conversion." It is designed as a resource book, but it is not one of those how-to-do-it manuals that promise to guide us simply through every step of a complicated process. Rather, it is intended to serve as a resource by broadening our horizons and deepening our understandings of conversion, the elusive and fascinating experience to which we minister with the *Rite of Christian Initiation of Adults* (RCIA).

In the decade since that Roman ritual book first appeared in its English translation, there has been a growing awareness that its implementation raises questions which touch on the most fundamental issues of Christian life. Communities that have begun to "do" the RCIA, at first usually unaware of its implications and its potential for renewal, have time and again found themselves challenged to reconsider just what it means today to be a Catholic Christian. There seems to be a dynamic—intrinsic to the pastoral effort at ministering to the conversion journey —which inevitably confronts those who minister with the same radical questions faced by the candidates themselves.

The conversion experience is like a many-faceted gem, seen as a thing of beauty when viewed from many different angles. The present volume's strength is the way in which it helps the reader to look upon that precious gem, catechumenal conversion, from several perspectives. We tend so often to stereotype the conversion experience, to have set ideas about what it is and how it happens. The many viewpoints represented by the essays in this volume constitute a powerful reminder that the mystery of human awakening to Divine Love is so rich that our understanding of it literally can never be exhausted. The resource offered here, then, is an invitation to a deeper understanding of a topic that is absolutely essential to the proper implementation of the RCIA. Those who minister to the conversion journey of others, or who are themselves caught up in such a journey, have need of clear understandings if they are to help rather than hinder the workings of God's grace.

The first essay by Louis Cameli underlines the vitally important role played by all who are in a caring relationship with a candidate for initiation. Father Cameli's background in spiritual theology allows him to bring to bear the rich tradition of ascetical teaching to which we Roman Catholics are heir. His clear, incisive exposition of some basic insights regarding spiritual transformation is shown to be immediately relevant to the catechumenal process. His individual focus, representative of most traditional teaching on spirituality, is complemented in the second essay by James Dunning's comments on the social dimensions of conversion. Probably more than any other person in this country at the present time, Dunning has taken the pulse of the actual situation of catechumenates across the nation. His lectures, workshops and writings have made him widely known and respected, and he brings great credibility to his contention that we must attend more closely to what he terms "four conversions with a social twist." His essay is both timely and provocative.

The third essay in this collection comes from the pen of a biblical scholar. For all of the rhetoric and interest in conversion that we have witnessed in recent years, there remains a remarkable absence of careful studies on the topic from the scriptural viewpoint. Michael Dick writes with the precision we have come to expect of a first-rate exegete, avoiding facile generalizations that make it appear there is only one biblical understanding of conversion. If the scriptural view of conversion is in some sense normative for our own understanding, then we can welcome the variety of perspectives that he demonstrates are enshrined in the Bible itself. Professor Dick's contribution is a strong reminder of how careful we must be in what we claim as the inspired understanding of conversion in the pages of the Jewish and Christian Scriptures.

Mark Searle writes from the standpoint of sacramental theology, and returns with some fresh insights to the familiar subject of the relationship between faith and sacrament. The theological depth with which he addresses these topics is impressive, but more striking yet is the clarity with which he shows their relevancy to the issue of conversion in the context of the RCIA. Our fifth essay by Regis Duffy is written from a similar perspective concerned with sacramental-liturgical issues. Developing approaches suggested by his book *Real Presence*, Father Duffy discusses the relationship between commitment and religious ritual, specifically as these questions surface in the catechumens' conversion journey and are celebrated with the rites of the RCIA. Edward Braxton represents the approach of systematic theology to the subject of conversion. His gift for popularization makes the highly technical views of Bernard Lonergan understandable to even the non-specialist.

Our two concluding essays introduce the reader to the world of the social sciences and their insights into the conversion experience. Robert Duggan surveys recent sociological literature and finds much there that is of interest to those involved in the conversion process celebrated in the RCIA. Romney Moseley, an associate of James Fowler at the Center for Faith Development, contributes a significant article reflecting current research among developmentalists. Despite its specialized nature, Dr. Moseley's essay raises some very practical issues for those overseeing the implementation of parish catechumenates. It will reward the effort required to follow his carefully nuanced discussion.

The RCIA directs that the catechumenal team, prior to the Rite of Election, deliberate and come to a decision regarding the candidates' level of conversion and their readiness to present themselves for full initiation at Easter. This awesome responsibility *must* be based on an informed and sensitive grasp of the many ways God's people can come to experience religious awakening. The candidates must be known deeply, and the nature of their conversion journeys must be such that the team can recognize and appreciate their richness. The present collection of essays hopes to contribute to that appreciation.

Caring for the Candidate: Insights of Spiritual Theology

Louis John Cameli

Introduction

People who want to care often find themselves with a question: How do I care? The large market of books on child care is built on that question. Parents want to attend, to help, to do well by their children. The exact shape of that attending, helping, and doing eludes them. They seek suggestions, resources that might "fill in" the gaps.

A similar situation, I believe, holds for those who want to implement the vision of the RCIA. Whether they are priests, deacons, professional religious educators, or laity, people who take the RCIA seriously want to care for the catechumens who are in the process of initiation. The urgency of caring gains momentum as those who are responsible in the Christian community realize the tender and vulnerable spot of those who are being initiated. For they are in the process of conversion, of change and transformation, a passage begun but not completed. And when we are in transit, we are vulnerable, tender, and in need of care. Then the question arises again: How to care for these people?

In this essay I would like to offer a perspective for caring. I come to the question from the viewpoint of spiritual theology. This branch of theological study, which some have defined as the science and art of the Christian experience, treats both the theoretical and the practical sides of Christian living. It can offer the person who wants to implement the vision of the RCIA a set of observations to help in the caring process. Spiritual theology can indicate areas of life and experience that need attending, and such an indication can guide the direction of care by giving some specific experiences to note.

Conversion and Relationship

Any remarks on caring for the person who is being initiated into the life of faith need to take into account the reality of conversion which is after all the heart of the initiation process. Other essays in this collection offer specific perspectives on the nature of conversion. Spiritual theology, too, has its own angle.

According to the framework of spiritual theology, conversion or the process of change and transformation is in function to the establishment of a new set of relationships. The RCIA itself speaks of the changing relationships into which the person enters. The relationships that are established or are changed are to Christ, to the Church, to oneself, to the world. The "General Introduction" to the rites of Christian Initiation speaks (number 2) of incorporation into Christ, formation into the people of God in the Church, and the witness of self as believer in the world as the terminal point of the entire process of initiation.

Relational language and perspectives are nothing new to Christian spirituality, even if the more contemporary framing of the language and perspectives is novel. The relational approach to understanding entrance into faith and the life of faith was, however, dimmed by a moralistic approach to spirituality in our recent past. In effect, this meant for many people until the renewal of Vatican II, and for some still today, a spirituality which is really a quantitative piety. Spirituality, for them, means doing religious things, the more things the better, and, in general, thereby becoming a "better" person.

In contrast, today we see the foundational relationship of our lives, that is, our relationship with God in Christ by the power of the Holy Spirit as a transforming relationship. More simply, we can say that to be in the relationship is to be in a process of transformation. There are some counterparts in human

experience which might help us to understand this unique relationship to God in Christ, into which catechumens are initiated.

Marriage relationships are transforming relationships.
When two people are in love and move beyond merely sharing
experiences to sharing a single life together, they are involved in
a transforming relationship. They cannot stay the same. They
reshape each other in their relationship. Specifics of this transformation emerge as we look at the partners on basic levels of
their lives. Physically, they find themselves transformed. Of
course, through their sexual experience they open up possibilities of body responses and sensitivities that are new and enhanc-
ing. They also care for each other physically, for example, in
terms of nutrition and shelter. Basic physical needs are met in
the relationship, and in meeting the needs, transformation happens.

There are other basic dimensions of human life that are
transformed in a marriage relationship. When two people love
each other, their perceptual capacities and their structures of
understanding are transformed. Are not love songs and the poetry of love the signs of a cognitive dimension of life that is
transformed because of a relationship? The relationship heightens certain awareness, enables a capacity to make connections,
and finally stimulates an intellectual kind of creativity.

On the level of feeling or affectivity there is obviously a
transformation that occurs because of the relationship. The
partners feel more closely, more intimately connected to each
other. The affective transformation does not, however, remain
limited by the relationship. The feelings spread outward. The
relationship offers possibilities of feeling differently about the
world, not simply about the other person. Automobile insur-
ance underwriters know this, when they are able to lower pre-
miums for married drivers who presumably have a calmer, more
settled feeling about themselves and the world.

Finally, the marriage relationship has a transforming impact on the values of the persons who are married. The values
which orient them to action undergo a transformation because
of their marital relationship. Specifically, this transformation

shows itself in many little ways, from time management, to
drinking patterns, to on-the-job performance. Things "are tak-
en" in a different way because of the relationship.

This detailed examination of a very human experience—a
loving marriage relationship—illustrates how relationships have
a transforming power in our lives. Now, if we can return to our
earlier considerations of the process of Christian initiation, we
can begin to see the process falling into a certain pattern. The
initiation process is a relational one, as the ritual itself indicates.
Catechumens are joined to Christ, to the Church, to the world
in a new way. As that relationship takes hold over the course of
the catechumenate with its various steps and stages, there is an
experience of conversion or transformation. The conversion
rooted in the new set of relationships manifests itself in three
principal dimensions of life: the cognitive or thinking side of
life, the affective or feeling side of life, and finally in the domain
of values that orient us to action.

In the remainder of this essay, I will take these three dimensions and indicate the particular shape of transformation which
might be occurring in the candidate for initiation. In effect, by
the end of the essay, we shall have named a list of areas of concern and experience for the candidate. Such a list can alert the
responsible persons of the Christian community to attend and
care for the candidates in the specific way that they may need
help in their passage, a time which we have already noted as
tender and vulnerable for them.

Cognitive Dimension

As the candidates move into a new set of relationships, as
those new relationships centered on incorporation in Christ exercise their transformative impact, issues and dimensions of the
cognitive side of life will inevitably surface.

The journeys of two men who frame fifteen hundred years
of Christian history, Augustine of Hippo and Thomas Merton,
are remarkable for their similarity on many points. One aspect
of their search is especially prominent. Their journeys as they
narrate them in *The Confessions* and in *The Seven Storey Mountain*

have very much to do with coming to a sense of coherence and meaning in life. In other words, a number of their questions as well as the markers of their conversion-initiation process had to do with coming to see the patterns and connections in life. They thirsted for intellectual coherence which could ground personal meaning. For Augustine, much of this quest centered on the relationship between good and evil and between the physical and the spiritual. Merton's search led him to try to piece together dependence and autonomy. In both cases, the search for coherence was part of a connective consciousness that grew correlatively to their coming into a fundamental relationship with God in Christ.

Another dimension of cognitive transformation rooted in a closer experience of relationship with God is the shattering of illusions and lies. The mind begins, because of the relationship with God as truth, to develop a critical consciousness about the self and the world. The ordinary talk of advertising, of popular values and amusement, of political manipulation no longer hold the same power. Idols of consumption and manipulation are destroyed. James Dunning's essay in this collection describes powerfully how this process works. We are walking in the domain of John's Gospel. There *alêtheia*, God's uncovering truth, lays bare the real emptiness of all idols. In this way, coming into the relationship with God means a transformation of critical consciousness. The intellectual-cognitive side of life is engaged with a new sharpness that comes from an experience of God's truth.

Still another aspect of transformed cognitive awareness is noted in no. 12 of the RCIA: ". . . the catechumens will learn . . . to be constant in the expectation of Christ in all things." This corresponds to a grace that is sought in the Ignatian tradition of spirituality—namely, to find Christ in all things. In effect, this amounts to a discerning consciousness. The discernment process is not simply a capacity to see, judge, and select among a number of options. Rather, it means the ability to discriminate and distinguish the complexities of life and to see within them the single, simple presence of the Lord. Discernment is both a gift given and a habit acquired. Radically a gift of God "who opens hearts," it is also something that grows with experience and practice, that is, with the application of the gift to the concrete circumstances of life.

The cognitive dimension of the transforming relationship generates another capacity, sometimes very marked in particular people. The relationship with God can bring a new way of seeing the world and the circumstances of people, a way that must be called creative. In other words, a gifted vision marks the believing person's perception of the world. It is not enough simply to see things as they are. The person who is caught in the love of God enjoys a creative sense of how things might be otherwise. This is the genius of a Vincent de Paul who is impelled by the love of Christ to think creatively about new approaches to the poor. It is the same kind of creative consciousness in love born of love that animated Mother Teresa of Calcutta to found the Missionary Sisters of Charity with their distinctive life style, and service rendered to the poor.

Such creativity bespeaks a new or, at least, a newly enlivened way of looking at the world, sifting through options, and coming to terms with possible practical strategies—all in situations that might to the "normal" eye seem impossible or collapsed under the weight of problems.

Serving the Cognitive Dimension
of Transformative Relationship

The various examples I have offered concern the ways that coming into a new relationship with God in Christ changes or converts the way we perceive, think, and understand. By simply being in the relationship, we cannot remain unchanged in our way of perceiving, thinking, and understanding. New or, at least, heightened forms of consciousness emerge in our lives. Connective consciousness enables us to piece together patterns and meaning in our lives and in the world. Critical consciousness assists us in "seeing through" the veil of illusions, half-truths, lies that block the simple and lucid presence of the Lord. A discerning consciousness allows us to discriminate and distinguish the movements of God in the many movements of life. Impelled by a persistent love, creative consciousness empowers us to look and see beyond the apparently collapsed possibilities of life to a new way and to a new thing that God does.

As the catechumens are brought into the new set of relationships with God in Christ and with the Church and with themselves, the mind of the person is touched and, eventually, transformed or converted. It should be clear that we are not talking simply about the intellectual journey into faith, the way, for example, that we might keep accumulating bits and pieces of religious detail to help us come to some conclusion about what we believe in. Nor are we simply talking about the intellectually interested person's journey into faith. It is neither data nor the propensities of a select few that are in play. We are, after all, human beings and therefore thinking beings. Whoever comes to faith and grows in faith does so with the gift of intellect, whatever the measure of the gift and however further refined it has become through educational development.

I know, for example, black women in Chicago who have been endowed with considerable native intelligence. The structures of society as they grew up gave them no opportunity to take their gifts and develop them through ordinary academic channels of education. Instead, their intelligence has been cultivated through a series of intense and trying life experiences. Through these, they have become highly educated people, although not in the academic understanding of that word.

They do not have the academically designated labels with which they can tag their experiences. They can, however, think and speak on deep levels. For example, these women make stringent demands in their thinking and reflection for patterns of meaning and coherence in life. They are not satisfied by pat or clichéd answers. Their critical consciousness has been sharpened to a point, so that they can pierce through structures of racism sustained by lies. Their discerning consciousness helps them to see the simple and essential elements of life in patterns of urban decay and otherwise bleak situations. Their creative consciousness has sparked concrete avenues of care and bonding that solidify human connections in fragile social matrices.

Someone who serves women such as these in their journey of faith, as perhaps they might make it through the RCIA, must be prepared to dialogue with them about the various dimensions of conversion that they will experience on a cognitive-intellectual level. The language and the jargon, even as it is employed in this essay, serve as a shorthand for those with a certain background. Such language and jargon is not only unnecessary but a real hindrance in serving these people. The realities signified by language are truly present. Anyone who aspires to serve such people must be ready to deal with this dimension of the transforming-converting relationship with God in Christ. But how can this be accomplished?

The ministry or serving that is to be offered is a ministry of *indication*. There is an obvious didactic dimension present in the RCIA. People need to be introduced to doctrines and practices and customs. This is a primarily informational and, in its own way, a formational activity. The slant here is different. As people are drawn into the transforming relationship with God in Christ, the primary task of the one serving the relationship is to indicate what is happening. They do not build the gift; it is given by God. The ministers or servants indicate or point out what is happening in terms of connective consciousness, critical consciousness, discerning consciousness, and creative consciousness. The assumption here is that the various ways of perceiving and understanding will take hold "automatically" as the relationship with God and the community intensifies and solidifies. A guide—whether sponsor, spiritual director, or whoever—is needed and provides an invaluable service by noting for the candidate in some explicit way what is happening.

Through this attention and through the indication, the candidate is enabled to own the elements of conversion and transformation that are a natural part of the perceptual and understanding or cognitive side of life.

Affective Dimension

The Christian spiritual tradition preserves for us a triple way of mysticism. There is the heady, intellectual mysticism of a Gregory of Nyssa, rooted in Neoplatonic philosophy. There is the action-oriented mysticism of a Dorothy Day. But there is also the feeling or affective mysticism of others, women especially like Julian of Norwich, a fourteenth century English hermitess, or Teresa of Avila, a sixteenth century Spanish Carmelite. The type of mysticism may follow the more dominant bent of the person toward the mind, toward action, or toward the heart. The inescapable fact, however, is that these elements are part of our lives and all parts (whatever the measure or proportion) enter into our religious experience.

It should be clear, then, that catechumens who are drawn more and more into a transforming relationship with God and the body of believers will also be touched to the heart by the experience. They will experience the transforming relationship, the conversion that takes hold of their lives, as an event of their affectivity or feelings.

The actual text of the RCIA does not speak with a highly noticeable language of affectivity or feelings. The language of mind and morals is far more in evidence. I would submit, however, that the level of affectivity is strongly, if not always explicitly, present in the text. The RCIA speaks of experiences such as eagerness, joy, bonding with the faith community, struggle. All this implies a rich weave of emotions that forms a backdrop for the rites of initiation. The liturgical books tend to a sober style of expression, not, I believe, because of a denial of emotion but because the emotions are so strong that the books achieve clearer definition and sharper focus through the use of "cool" language.

Because of the emotional sobriety of the liturgical texts, a special and valuable characteristic of the Roman Rite, the spiritual-theological tradition can be of assistance in "filling out" the picture of the conversion and transformation process. Spiritual theology can draw on the testimony of the affective experience of believers, especially as this crystallizes in the lives of some people of significant spiritual experience.

For example, St. Teresa of Avila writes about spiritual experience with clarity and intellectual depth. The experience she describes, however, is richly textured with many different emotional or affective registers. I think that she can be of help to us in noting some of the key affective dimensions of becoming involved in a transforming relationship with God in Christ and through the Church.

A good starting point is the very simple definition-description of prayer which she offers in her autobiography. "To my mind," she says, "mental prayer is nothing else than dealing with friendship, taking time frequently to be alone with the one we know who loves us." Contained within this description of prayer is a whole approach to God as intimate love. The affective or feeling dimension of prayer is prominent, because the prayer experience she speaks of does not have some target or goal besides itself. The reality of mental prayer for St. Teresa is to rest in friendship with the one we know who loves us. The emphasis falls on being connected and bonded and sensing that. This accurately describes one person's experience of the affective side of being in a transformative relationship with God.

Another side of the affective dimension of Teresa's experience emerges in her sense of claims and belonging. Throughout her autobiography, she struggles with her sense of belonging to God and of God belonging to her. The language of her love of God includes the language of claims. God has claimed her, she has claimed God. In her experience of feeling a belonging and a being claimed, Teresa gives additional testimony to the affective side or resonance of her life of faith, of being in relationship with God.

Interestingly, Teresa is very cautious about her religious experiences. She seeks to test them. She continually submits them to the judgment of the Church. Part of her motivation is her desire not to be deceived by feelings, a legitimate concern at any time and especially in the rarefied mystical climate of her sixteenth century Spain. There is, however, an additional motivation for submitting her experiences to the Church. She believes that her experience of belonging and of being claimed by God is mediated through the Church. Her sensible experience is not only an interior affect that touches her from the inside, but a connection and bondedness that also comes from the outside through her participation in the life of the Church. So, she expresses what we can call the ecclesial mediation of the experience of God—but on a level of feeling, the feeling of belonging and of being claimed.

Earlier we noted that there is a very rich texture to the emotions and the entire life of feeling that Teresa relates as she speaks of her relationship with God in its more direct and in its mediated experiences. One way of noting the texture of her emotional or affective life in her life of faith is to see a weave of emotions, affect moving in different directions. Her autobiography, for example, bears the marks of laughter and tears, loss and gain, departure and arrival, remorse and joy, wrenching and joining. The dialectic of emotions which Teresa experiences are simply the expression of a life of intense relationship with God. Such a life will incorporate—just as the Gospels do—a very full range of emotion.

Often, readers of Teresa's autobiography are struck by her expressions of "negative" emotion. She speaks of hesitation, of sadness, of a sense of her own disordered passion. Readers are impressed by these expressions, because they dare to indicate a range of religious experience which is beyond "the nice." In the contrast between her finite being and God's infinity, between her sin and God's surpassing grace, between her darkness and God's unapproachable light, there is bound to be a set of negative emotions. These emotions are simply the expression of the gap between the creature and the Creator, between the sinner and the All Holy One.

The other emotional strain that strikes readers forcefully is Teresa's experience and expression of ecstatic union with God. Elation comes from surrender into a sensed and total love. It forms an experience which races ahead of her ability to express it. The imagery she employs sometimes shocks because of its intensity, as, for example, when she uses the sexual metaphor of dying and living in an act of intimate union.

Teresa of Avila's relationship with God is a transforming relationship. It transforms her on many levels of life. Here, we have noted the effect of this relationship on her affective or emotional life. She both experiences and expresses an intensity of feeling that will often surprise us, sometimes shock us, and always cause us to consider the emotional dimensions of our own relationship with the Lord in his Church.

Serving the Affective Dimension
of the Transforming Relationship

Teresa of Avila represents all who are on a conscious and committed pilgrimage of faith, people who actively seek to develop and deepen their relationship with the Lord. Her experience—seen as we have seen it from the angle of affectivity—provides us with some indications for people who are just beginning their journey. In fact, for catechumens who make the basic transition in the conversion process of the RCIA, Teresa's emotional experience can cast some light. A feel for her journey can also assist those who serve the affective dimension of the people in a process of conversion to relationship with the Lord in his Church.

Catechumens in the conversion process not only learn new things and a new relationship, they also enter into a new world of feeling because of their new relationship with the Lord in the Church. Just as for Teresa, catechumens may find the emotional dimension especially clear and prominent in the initial explorations of prayer. Teresa, recall, experienced prayer as presence in friendship, a shared intimacy with the "one we know who loves us." A true "revolution in feeling" can occur for persons who begin to come in contact with the one who is the mystery and origin of the universe as a "friendly presence." To move in prayer from a sense of distance to immediate intimacy with the one who ties together our origin and destiny of our lives will necessarily have a strong emotional impact upon us.

For Teresa, her developing experience of being in relationship with God in and through the Church brought with it a sense of belonging as well as a sense of being claimed. Catechumens who are introduced into the community of faith, especially if they have not known a sense of community on the scale of a Church, will feel with particular intensity the new sense of belonging. They can also begin to come to terms with the double direction of claims: they can make claims on the Church to which they belong and the Church can, in turn, make claims on them.

All relationships which are intimate and intense carry within themselves the possibilities for a whole set of dialectical feelings, polarities of emotion which accompany the development of all significant relationships. The mix for Teresa of tears and laughter, departure and arrival, loss and gain, remorse and joy, wrenching and joining does not belong to Teresa alone. Catechumens who are moving into a similar relationship with the Lord in the Church will also experience the same full range of feelings. They contain within themselves the seeds of laughter and tears and all the other emotional experiences touched and triggered by a significant relationship.

The negative feelings generated by her developing relationship with God played an important role for Teresa. They mirror the passage she makes across a "gap"—between sin and grace, finitude and infinity, darkness and light. Catechumens as they enter the new relationship with God in the Church also experience the struggle and the resistances and the pain that accompany their passage into a new realm of relationship.

The joy of union, startling in its intensity and placed so prominently in the religious experience of Teresa, also forms part of the experience of the catechumens in their conversion process. As they enter into relationship with the Lord in the Church, their sense of being brought together, united, will inevitably and, at times, prominently involve feelings of joy in union.

The person who serves catechumens moving through the process of initiation must attend to the affective or emotional side of their experience. In attending to the cognitive or intellectual side of the initiation process, we noted the need to inform and teach as well as the need to indicate what was happening on that intellectual level. Service to the affective dimension will be shaped somewhat differently.

The persons serving catechumens' affective life as they enter into a transforming relationship with God in the Church provide a very simple yet crucial service. Their ministry can be

indicated in three words: *identifying, accepting,* and *accompanying.*
They identify the feelings or the affective resonance that is alive
and at work in the catechumens. Identifying the feelings is a
simple process, but a particularly valuable one for the catechumens. To feel is to be caught up in emotion whatever it might
be. To hear someone identify a feeling is to be able to accept, to
locate it within the wider currents of life, and—perhaps most
importantly—to know that we have been understood.

A second service to be rendered to the catechumens is to accept their feelings as they go through the initiation process. At
first, it may seem that the negative feelings are the ones that
need "outside acceptance," so that it might be permissible to
have them. In fact, this is true, but it is not the only question.
The positive feelings, for example of belonging and elation, also
need to be accepted. A strong positive feeling, especially one of
those connected with religion or other areas of experience that
might be considered "exotic," needs to be accepted and integrated as a genuine and real piece of the whole experience of coming
into relationship with God in the Church.

Finally, catechumens need others to accompany them on
the feeling level as they progress through the process of initiation. Accompaniment means simply to walk in solidarity with
them. There is no need to add anything, to critique experience,
but simply to walk with the person on the level of feeling.

Dimension of Values
That Lead to Commitment and Action

Significant relationships have a transformative impact on
us on many deep levels of life. We saw that that is the case in
marriage. We have begun to spell it out in the process of initiation. We have already noted at least two levels of human life that
are touched and somehow transformed, the cognitive and the affective. In this final section, we will explore a third level of life:
valuing that orients us to make commitments and to take action.

Once Augustine and Thomas Merton passed a threshold in
their conversion process, they not only knew things differently
and felt differently about them, they also set about reorganizing

their lives to reflect the new set of values they had begun to embrace. They could no longer simply stay in the world and work, for example, as if there had been no change in their heart, no relationship that claimed them and which they themselves claimed as precious and central to their lives. Shifting the investment of their time, money, and energy, as well as the reorganization of their life style, reflected the impact of their new relationship with God on their value system.

One particularly dramatic way in which the relationship with God reshapes the values, the commitments, and the actions of people is found in the spirituality of martyrdom. The age of the martyrs is not limited simply to the first four centuries of the Christian era. Every age has had its martyrs. In our own day, the martyrs include Martin Luther King, Jr., Oscar Romero, and the three women missioners slain in El Salvador in 1981. These people found themselves engaged in a relationship with God both in an immediate and in a mediated way through other people. Not only did they perceive things differently because of their relationship, not only did they feel things differently because of their relationship, they valued things differently and so were prepared to commit themselves and act differently. The proof of this is in the transparent witness of their death. For in laying down their lives they give ample and unambiguous testimony that among their values, life on earth was subordinate to higher values of justice, peace, and love which stemmed from their relationship with God.

The synthesis or integration of the cognitive and affective dimensions of the relationship with God in values and action is best captured in a phrase characteristic of the spirituality of Ignatius of Loyola. In its original Latin it reads: *contemplativus in actione.* The literal English translation would render it as: "a contemplative in action." The ideal in Ignatian spirituality is to embody the contemplative stance, that is, a discerning and feeling sense of God rooted in prayer *precisely within* the course of action, of commitment, of larger service to the world. The relationship with God, in this perspective, is in a circular relationship with one's relationships with other persons. Love of God and love of neighbor are not competing values, but one value with two sides which fund each other and find their integration in the life of an individual on the level of values translated into commitments and action.

When people are touched by their relationship with God—touched in a deep and lasting way—what they value and what they prize is transformed. Life style may be reorganized around new priorities. Life itself becomes relative to higher values. The pursuit in commitment and action is the God who is contemplated therein.

Serving Values Transformed by the Transforming Relationship

When catechumens follow the course of initiation, they enter into a new and transforming relationship. As the cognitive and affective level settled in the process, their question echoes the crowds in Jerusalem after Peter's Pentecost speech: "Brothers, what must we do?" (Acts 2:37). A desire flows quite naturally from any significant relationship that has an impact on us. It is a desire *to do* something. That desire is a complex synthesis of felt conviction (affective and cognitive levels) which has come to prize the object of conviction (values) and wishes to act expressively and constructively on the basis of those values.

People who care for the catechumens need to attend to the emergence of a new value system and the drive to form a new set of commitments, as well as the strong desire to embody those values and commitments in action. Three words describe what, I believe, can be offered to the catechumens: *encouragement, moderation,* and *support.*

Catechumens need encouragement as new values and a new value system begin to crystallize in their lives. The reorganization of priorities, the shifting of priorities, the orientation of action, all may run counter to patterns familiar to the catechumens and ordinarily supported by their culture.

Moderation is a necessary ingredient in the process. A kind of moderation that comes from without is especially helpful. A rush of enthusiasm can spend itself quickly and unproductively.

A voice that counsels patience, steadiness, and reflective action will serve persons who find themselves in a transforming relationship very well.

Support differs from encouragement which is given more personally. Support involves the creation of an environment of trust where values may be tested, commitments may be pronounced, and actions may be tried. The catechumens who grapple with their newly emerging values and commitments and styles of action need a climate within which they can let these take root.

When, for example, catechumens begin to relate with Christ our justice, who came to reconcile all things in himself, a powerful direction is set in motion. In contemporary terms, the issues of justice and peace may achieve a new prominence and a heightened urgency. The values, the commitments, the actions that flow from this experience need a ministering community to offer encouragement, moderation, and support.

Conclusion

We began this essay with a question: How to care for candidates who enter the process of initiation? In other words, how can we serve candidates who have entered a process of conversion? What does spirituality or spiritual theology have to offer?

Our considerations have focused on a very narrow band of experience. Still, that band is central to the entire process of initiation. For we took the initiation process and the conversion which it implies to be a time of coming into a new and transforming relationship. By drawing on the analogy of a single and simple and transforming relationship in marriage, we began to see the areas of implication for those who are in the process of initiation. At least three significant dimensions of life are touched and transformed in that relationship: the cognitive or thinking side of life, the affective or feeling side of life, and the valuing side of life that leads us to make commitments and take action.

According to the perspective of spiritual theology, certain

"points" of impact or experience emerge with clarity in the lives of those who are being initiated. When the ministers of the community are aware of these, they can better attend to them.

Finally, although we have paid very little attention to this aspect because of the limitations of space, something else very significant is to be noted. The community that attends and serves the initiation of candidates into a transforming relationship with the Lord in the Church are themselves grasped by the same loving and transforming relationship. As they serve others, they become aware of a single relationship that binds all to him in whom all things hold together until God becomes all in all. They themselves are blessed who prepare paths for the Lord's blessing.

Confronting the Demons: The Social Dimensions of Conversion

James B. Dunning

In Flannery O'Connor's short story, "Revelation," Mrs. Turpin lived in a neat, tidy world, where everyone had a place. In her hierarchy, most places were below hers: niggers (as she called them), then white-trash, then home-owners, then home-and-land-owners like herself. For that world, she constantly cried, "Thank you, Jesus, for making everything the way it is!"

One afternoon that world came clattering down. In a doctor's office, after Mrs. Turpin had explained how she thanked Jesus, an ugly girl hurled a book and spat these words at her, "Go back to hell where you came from, you old wart hog!"

That night, after washing down wart hogs, now her namesake, she stood looking at them.

> Until the sun slipped finally behind the tree line, Mrs. Turpin remained there with her gaze bent to (the hogs) as if she were absorbing some abysmal life-giving knowledge. At last she lifted her head. There was only a purple streak in the sky, cutting through a field of crimson and leading, like an extension of the highway, into the descending dusk. . . . A visionary light settled in her eyes. She saw the streak as a vast swinging bridge extending upward from the earth through a field of living fire. Upon it a vast horde of souls were rumbling toward heaven. There were whole companies of white-trash, clean for the first time in their lives, and

23

bands of black niggers in white robes, and battalions of freaks and lunatics shouting and clapping and leaping like frogs. And bringing up the end of the procession was a tribe of people whom she recognized at once as those who, like herself, had always had a little of everything and the God-given wit to use it right.... They were marching behind the others with great dignity, accountable as they had always been for good order and common sense and respectable behavior. They alone were on key. Yet she could see by their shocked and altered faces that even their virtues were being burned away.[1]

Once again a pharisee thanks God that she is not sinful like the rest of humankind, especially that publican over there; but once again publicans strut up the yellow-brick road into the Kingdom. Once again conversion is not just for "converts" but for all who look at wart hogs and the sky and hear a call from the Lord to change our hearts, literally to break our hearts.

The shock demolished Mrs. Turpin because the revelation shattered her taken-for-granted world. Mrs. Turpin since the day of her birth had breathed in the air of a consumerist culture where home-and-land-owners were kings and queens of the mountain. The evils are not private but systemic, built into the system, as American as apple pie. Too much talk of conversion is narrowed to a private, born-again, Jesus-and-me experience blind to the social evils which enslave us.

Original sin is not just the disobedience of our first parents. It is precisely these evils engendered by all parents. Every child is born into evils which she has not produced but which infect her and deflect her from the poverty of spirit, fullness of mercy, thirst for justice, and peace making which Jesus proclaims in the reign of God.

These evils are the real demons of our times. We can certainly believe in personal evil spirits, but we should not reduce the demonic to cute little red devils perched on Flip Wilson's shoulder ("The devil made me do it!") or to nasty little girls spewing forth green vomit in *The Exorcist*. The Judaeo-Christian experience of the demonic also reveals that there is evil in us which is more than us, not self-produced but the product of an entire culture. We might call these the "isms": consumerism, militarism, racism, sexism, nationalism, privatism, clericalism, fatalism. They are woven into the very fabric of our American culture. Any approach to conversion which purports to offer healing in the real world seriously betrays the Gospel if it does not confront these demons which oppose the reign of God.

Let me be clear. I am not on a "hate America" campaign. I believe there is more grace than dis-grace in the American people. But if we are faithful to our prophetic tradition which proclaims that everything human is touched by fragility and evil, we need to stand before our non-prophet organizations to exorcise and heal. There is much that is anti-Christ and anti-Gospel in our culture which blocks conversion. As Pope John Paul said when he was Cardinal Wojtyla:

> We are now standing in the face of the greatest historical confrontation humanity has gone through. I do not think that wide circles of the American society or wide circles of the Christian community realize this. We are now facing the final confrontation between ... the Gospel versus the anti-Gospel.[2]

In a world where militarism means the possibility of nuclear holocaust and consumerism means gobbling up resources like Pac-Man, no treatment of conversion should reduce it to a private, born-again experience and neglect its social dimensions. Conversion which stops with "Jesus and me" is abortive. It stops where Jesus does not stop. He calls us to journey with him to the Kingdom.

That is the good news. Evil is a social affair, but so also are grace and conversion. It is a community affair. Conversion is entering a community in which the giddy grace of God is enfleshed. Grace is God's presence. God chooses to be present through the support and challenge of a community which is non-consumerist, non-racist, non-militaristic, non-sexist. God gifts that community with the Spirit who heals the isms and exorcises the evil spirits.

I stress this because too much talk about justice and social responsibility leaves us guilty and powerless. If we stop with the bad news that evil is more than my private production, that is a neat way to avoid responsibility. The good news is that goodness is also more than us. Goodness is God, and goodness is incarnate in Jesus and all touched by his Spirit. Conversion discovers the power of that goodness which is more than us and which can heal the wounds inflicted by the demons. Healing comes, then, not through the language of guilt or despair nor rage and cheap grace but through both the language of grief and compassion and also hope which releases the genuine power of people created in God's image.

In fact, Genesis 1:26–28 which proclaims us as God's images is both challenge and support for the call to social conversion. It is challenge because every person created in God's image has a right to the basic resources which allow co-creation, with power to be fruitful and multiply. It is support and grounds for our hope because images of God are empowered to confront the demons. The world's bishops alluded to that power in the Synod in 1971. They said they were

> able to perceive the serious injustices which are building around the world . . . a network of domination, oppression and abuses which stifle freedom and which keep the greater part of humanity from sharing in the building up and enjoyment of a more just and more fraternal world. . . . In the face of the present-day situation of the world, marked as it is by the grave sin of injustice, we recognize both our responsibility and our inability to overcome it by our own strength. Such a situation urges us to listen with a humble and open heart to the word of God, as he shows us new paths toward action in the cause of justice in the world.[3]

I have called that "network of domination" the demonic in our culture. To exorcise those demons I offer four conversions with a social twist:

From Pac-Man Consumerism to Poverty and Gift
From Navel-Observatory Privatism to Mission and
  Church
From American Way Nationalism to the Kingdom of God
  in Covenant
From Doomsday Fatalism to Liberating Hope

From Pac-Man Consumerism to Poverty and Gift

Listen to the messages from Madisonavenueland about salvation: Datsun saves. K-Mart is your saving place. Buick is
something to believe in. GE brings good things to life. How to
wrap your package?—Warner's Bra. A heart to heart talk with
Climatrol Computer. Coke is the real thing. Love is Musk.

No wonder Mrs. Turpin gets the message: salvation is for
home-and-land-owners, and owners of Datsuns, computers,
Musk, and Warner's bras who with voracious appetites gobble
up the earth like Pac-Man. Even though Gallup claims that
ninety percent of us believe in God, who is the American God?
How much of this is what Robert Bellah calls a "civil religion,"
not releasing energies in society for the reign of God but har-
nessing the Gospel for the American way? As Calvin Coolidge
said, the American way means that the business of America is
business. Do Jesus and the reign of God drive business toward
salvation, or do Datsun and Buick drive Jesus?

Confrontation between the Gospel and the idols and demons of business began early. Remember the silversmith Demetrius in the Acts of the Apostles who made miniature shrines of
Artemis and provided jobs for the neighborhood.

> "Men," he said, "you know that our prosperity de-
> pends on this work. But as you can see and hear for
> yourselves ... this Paul has persuaded great numbers
> of people to change their religion. He tells them that
> man-made gods are no gods at all. The danger grows,
> not only that our trade will be discredited, but even
> that the temple of the greatest goddess Artemis will
> count for nothing" (Acts 19:25–27).

Demetrius still hawks his wares on prime-time TV, up to twenty-seven percent of which can be given to advertising, consuming about three years of an average lifetime. Who can resist such a bombardment of consumerism, competition, hoarding, unnecessary waste, planned obsolescence? Fifty billion dollars a year is not spent on advertising for no payoff. The demons begin to possess the average pre-kindergartener who spends sixty-four percent of waking time watching television game shows (devoted to unmitigated greed and competition), soap operas (where the competition is for bodies and bedrooms), cartooned violence sponsored by junk foods, and commercials convincing them that life has no meaning without Atari and Pac-Man, without mainlining on materialism.

We aren't even satisfied with infecting our own children. For example, Nestle felt bound to sell the third world on infant formula which people did not need, could not afford, and didn't know how to use.

What is so demonic about all this? Some of us really come to believe that "Datsun saves," not Jesus. Salvation is equated with *products*, not *persons*, especially persons like the elderly, the handicapped, prisoners, the poor, the unborn who don't produce. Genesis called us to be fruitful and multiply. Paradoxically, we sometimes honor the creations, the products, rather than the "imago Dei" who creates. The persons themselves become expendable before the consuming idols of competition, vested interest, and planned obsolescence. That is why the demon consumerism, which generates our need to gather power at the expense of others, can open the door for the other demons: racism, sexism, ageism, militarism, nationalism, clericalism.

John Kavanaugh writes:

> Once a man or woman, be he or she oppressor or oppressed, whether dressed in silk or sprawled in a Calcutta slum, whether on a battlefield or in a delivery room, whether bourgeoisie or proletariat, whether criminal, president, or both, is perceived as a thing or in terms of the commodity, he or she is thereby rendered replaceable. The fetus is a "blob of protoplasm."

The criminal is "scum and vermin." The brain-damaged are "vegetables." The poor are "like animals." . . . Only on this level of understanding can the questions of violence in the street or among nations, on death row or in hospitals, be adequately addressed as fragmented symptoms of a totality which itself so often escapes our attention and critique.[4]

I admit I speak as no casual observer of violence, but as a victim of several muggings during the past few years no doubt perpetrated by one whose adrenalin was in part charged by the consumerism of prime-time TV.

Jesus proclaims that our treasure is where our heart is. Jesus puts his heart with the poor. The heart of the beatitudes in Matthew and this solidarity with the poor in Luke is Jesus' spirituality grounded on Isaiah 61:

The spirit of the Lord God is upon me,
  because the Lord has anointed me;
He has sent me to bring glad tidings to the lowly,
  to heal the brokenhearted,
To proclaim liberty to the captives
  and release to the prisoners,
To announce a year of favor from the Lord
  and a day of vindication by our God . . . (Is. 61:1–2).

As far as we can tell Jesus was born into the middle class. He made himself poor to identify with the poor, to enter compassion with the poor. He calls us to share the treasure in his heart. He invites all "rich young men" (and women) to sell what they have and give to the poor.

Pope John Paul II echoed that same invitation for Americans:

Within the framework of your national institutions and in cooperation with all your compatriots, you will also want to seek out the structural reasons which foster or cause the different forms of poverty in the world and in your own country. . . . The poor of the United States and of the world are your brothers and sisters in Christ. You must never be content to leave them just the crumbs from the feast. You must take of your substance, and not just of your abundance, in order to help them. And you must treat them like guests at your family table.[5]

If there are structural reasons in our national institutions that cause poverty, then personal conversion will not heal our ills. We shall need political and economic skills. This is not the place to enter that analysis. Personal conversion, however, which grounds us in a Gospel spirituality of poverty of spirit is that which moves us to solidarity with the poor so that we might find the skills. More than any other conversion we Americans need to change from Pac-Man consumerism to poverty and the experience of life as gift.

More than anything else, the good news that we do not save and Datsun does not save but salvation is the free gift of God in Jesus to our poverty exorcises the American demon consumerism. That is the healing good news for Marlboro men and women of true grit, Horatio Algers who lift themselves up by their bootstraps, who believe that God helps those who help themselves.

We exorcise not to reveal our guilt but to reveal our poverty—our absolute dependence on God for healing. Only those can be liberated who *know* they are enslaved. Only those who know they have been self-possessed, idol-possessed, demon-possessed can be possessed by the Holy Spirit. Only those who know they stand in need can receive a gift and then share it. Only those who come up empty can receive the gift of God's fullness. Only those who have nothing can receive everything.

That is the key message of the Hebrew Scriptures. The Lord God calls the ungifted. Everyone knows that Noah hit the bottle and Abraham was too old to have a child. Even Sarah laughs, "You old fool! Where am I going to have it—the geriatric ward? Who's going to pay for it—Medicare?" Everyone knows you could trust Esau the reliable, not Jacob the trickster and heel. Everyone knows Moses had a lisp, and that the prophets were a ragged lot of mad hatters, with Isaiah too sinful of lips (so God gives him hot lips), Jeremiah too young in years, Gideon too bored and boring. Everyone knew that Ruth was too Gentile to have a kid from a classy family tree, and Mary was too virginal to give birth from that tree.[6] In the Hebrew Scriptures the message is: God enters our poverty with gift.

That is also the hallmark of the stories in the Christian Scriptures: only the empty can be filled by God. To whom does Jesus announce the Kingdom? Nathan Mitchell says it was to

> the misfits, the unworthy, the "uglies." The kingdom was for sinners, tax-collectors, lepers, prostitutes, and club-foots; it was a kingdom for the messy and the miserable.... Instead of being a towering cedar of Lebanon, the kingdom Jesus preached was like a scrawny mustard plant. Instead of being the Chase Manhattan Bank, the kingdom was like a poor old woman who lost a dime and swept her house all day until she found it. Instead of being a dramatic "close encounter of the third kind," the kingdom was as hidden and humble as a bit of yeast in a batch of dough.[7]

The Father of Jesus is forever running down roads to meet prodigal sons and daughters and throwing them parties, outrageously overpaying workers in vineyards, scurrying around searching for lost sheep, hearing the prayers of publican-sinners not pharisee-saints like Mrs. Turpin. He is

> an eccentric host who, when the country-club crowd's calendar is full, goes out into the skid rows and soup kitchens and charity wards and brings home a freak show. The man with no legs who sells shoelaces at the corner. The old woman in the moth-eaten fur coat who makes her daily rounds of garbage cans. The old wino with his pint in a brown paper bag.... The candles are

all lit, and the champagne glasses filled. At a sign from the host, the musicians in their gallery strike up "Amazing Grace."[8]

Grace. In Latin, *gratia*—gift. To receive a gift—that is the basic message of all these stories of our people. That is why Bernard Lonergan identifies the heart of all conversion as the shift from life as problem-to-be-solved to life as mystery-and-gift-to-be-savored. More than anything else, that is what we seek when discerning conversion. Do we yearn for self-made perfection or God-given election? Is life reward for our virtue (with Mrs. Turpin) or gift to our poverty, one damn thing after another or (as one wag told me) one damn gift after another?

If we turn to a faith that shares God's vision of us, we turn from the demon consumerism which equates salvation with what we have to a valuing of every person for who we are— mysteries and gifts of infinite worth, images of God whose every hair is numbered, worth more than many sparrows. With less products for consumption in our warehouse, God can fill us with gift. This does not get at the systemic demons infecting our culture which demand social conversion. But it is the beginning of social conversion because the marvelous thing is that gifts are not for hoarding, competing, vested interests, and greedy consumption. Gifts are for-giving. We give gifts away. As Karl Rahner says (in a somewhat sexist translation), "Man only *is* when he gives himself away."

From Navel-Observatory Privatism to Mission and Church

Beetle Bailey is standing guard duty at night. He hears a noise and shouts, "Halt, who goes there?" Back comes the response, "Ah, how often have I asked myself that very question! Is it possible to face yourself and know who you are, or is the pain of self-discovery just too much? Aristotle says, 'Know thyself.' Easy, you say—but Oh, what a tangled web we weave to hide from that self-knowledge! So I say to you—I am Plato, no more and no less—a live, breathing participant in the game of life." Beetle Bailey groans, "Now I know why they don't give us live ammunition out here!"

For many, the 1970's were a decade of navel-gazing, looking in the mirror and asking, "Who am I?" I belonged to a generation of catechists who prodded adolescents to ask that question. They peered long and hard into that mirror searching for self, and all they found were pimples and acne.

Researcher Daniel Yankelovich has called this the inner trip of self-discovery and self-fulfillment which marked the 1970's and still marks the 1980's. It is a time of both personal and social isolationism, narcissism, relativism which was perhaps an understandable reaction to the activism of the 1960's.

In the churches the navel-gazing and narcissism sometimes focuses not just on the individual. It might still focus inward on "the group"—our groovy marriage, our groovy renewed parish, our swinging charismatic or cursillo group. It is community ("koinonia") cut off from evangelization and outreach ("diakonia").

In a narcissistic time conversion can mean born-again in Jesus, preaching Jesus but not the kingdom of justice and freedom which he preached. Jim Wallis writes:

> By neglecting the kingdom of God in our preaching, we have lost the integrating and central core of the gospel. The disastrous result is "saved" individuals who comfortably fit into the old order while the new order goes unannounced. The social meaning of conversion is lost and a privatized gospel supports the status quo. ... Listening to evangelistic preachers today, one might never know that the coming of Jesus was intended to turn the world upside down.[9]

Christian faith affirms: I know myself not in the navel but in relationship to the Other and the others. If discovered in isolation, my story can be bad news, because I find primarily my own evil, sin, fragility. My story finds meaning in the community of fellow-travelers who journey toward Emmaus together and discover who they are in the midst of the death-resurrection story of Jesus. Again, conversion begins by discovering more than myself. It means discovering the *gift* of God in Christ Jesus who calls us to for-giving—to give the gifts away.

This second social dimension of conversion leads us a step farther. We move through the experience of gift to the call to mission out of which we become not just Church as community but Church as servant. That's how it happened with Jesus. First came *gift*—the good news of God's love which gifts us in his Spirit with poverty of spirit, fullness of mercy, thirst for justice, peacemaking. Then comes *mission*—"Go, therefore, make disciples of all nations. Baptize them in the name of the Father and of the Son and of the Holy Spirit, and teach them to observe all the commands I gave you. And know that I am with you always; yes, to the end of time" (Mt 28:19–20). *Then* comes *Church*—believers find the ministries, the forms, the institutions which serve the mission.

The demon privatism, narcissism, threatens to make Church the idol. Church *has* a mission, in the sense that the Church possesses the mission, defines the terms of mission, and begins to minister in ways that make mission serve the Church. That can happen when in an effort to adapt to a culture the Church loses its soul to the culture, e.g., when clericalism becomes the ecclesiastical version of sexism and the power and control of a male-dominated culture. Or the Church can lose its soul to the ideologies of a culture and identify its mission with serving cultural nationalism ("Kill a Commie for Christ!") or counter-cultural rebellion ("Throw the bomb in the name of Jesus!").

But even in the "best" of churches mission can subtly shift toward serving the Church, toward self-maintenance, toward "churchy" ministries which serve our groovy parish rather than build the Kingdom of justice and peace with those outside our swinging group. We certainly rejoice in shared ministries: eucharistic ministers, ministers of the word, social ministries from St. Vincent de Paul Societies to Pax Christi, catechists and spiritual directors. But what of the basic call of the Church to help lay people discern their gifts and send them on mission not just to Church meetings of the institution but into their lives where most people are called to be Church: as parents and singles, in work and in the arts, as old people and young, in politics and economics, in the cities and in the country? That is the conversion which moves us from both personal and ecclesiastical navel-gazing to mission and the Church as servant. That is the Church which will confront and heal the isms.

There is hope that the catechumenate process of the Rite of Christian Initiation of Adults will call new Christians to that kind of Church. The jargon today is that we are all called to mission by baptism. It is interesting that the catechumenate died in the third and fourth centuries when people lost that sense of universal mission. The demon clericalism moved into the vacuum, and people went to abbeys and novitiates if they wanted to become "real" Christians and enter into mission. We have come full circle. The catechumenate process leads up to Pentecost when each new Christian celebrates his or her gifts and pledges them to mission, especially in the streets and marketplaces. That is a Church grounded on an ecclesiology and ecclesiastical physiology centered not on navels but on feet: "How beautiful are the feet of those who bring good news!" (Rom 10:15). That Church has patience with shy people who shudder at bringing the good news only as extroverts. That Church challenges shy people, however, beyond a "Jesus and me" privatism to the mission of somehow responding to the call to social responsibility.

From American Way Nationalism
to the Kingdom of God in Covenant

Perhaps more than any other demon, nationalism (often coupled with racism) testifies to the failure of religion to convert minds and hearts. Too often nation and race and culture have converted religion to their cause rather than religion converting the nation. In the name of the Lord God, with self-righteous fury the battles rage between Hebrews and Canaanites, Christians and Hebrews, Christians and Turks in the Crusades, French and English in Canada, Protestant and Catholic in Northern Ireland, Arabs and Jews, Christians and Moslems in

Lebanon. I recall a film which portrayed the Anglican bishop invoking the blessing of the "royalist God" on the troops on one side of the valley while Oliver Cromwell called upon the powers of the "populist God" on the opposite side. Not only royalists and populists were slaughtered in the ensuing battle; we also witnessed the death of God. God must share the "conscientious objection" of many young people at being drafted into so many armies.

Our own country was founded with a vibrant biblical faith that envisioned our founding mothers and fathers as a new people of God, on exodus into a new promised land which offered liberty and justice for all in a new covenant between God and the people. That vision has brought freedom and untold blessings for millions of people. It has not meant liberty and justice *for all*. We founded this nation on broken promises to the original inhabitants of this great land. The Revolutionary period granted rights only to white, male land-owners. The Civil War sought to extend those rights beyond the white middle-class. Robert Bellah claims that our own times clamor for Americans to smash the idols of nationalism and extend those blessings beyond our national boundaries.

> We live at present in a third time of trial at least as severe as those of the Revolution and the Civil War.... It is a test of whether republican liberty established in a remote agrarian backwater of the world in the 18th century shall prove able or willing to confront successfully the age of mass society and international revolution. It is a test of whether we can control the very economic and technical forces, which are our greatest achievement, before they destroy us.[10]

Bellah concludes, "The inward reform of conversion, the renewal of an inward covenant among the remnant that remains faithful to the hope for rebirth, is more necessary than it has ever been in America."[11]

That is why it would be the height of irresponsibility not to challenge Americans in our times of nuclear fright and economic interdependence to ponder the dimensions of a social conversion which moves us beyond narrow nationalism. Biblical conversion has always eschewed "space cadets" out of touch with earthy, messy, concrete historical events in space and time which happen not just to individuals but to a people. Conversion happens not in some historical vacuum but to a poeple enslaved in Egypt, exiled in Babylon, oppressed by Persia, taxed by Rome. God calls into history and grants his covenants: "You saw what I, the Lord, did to the Egyptians and how I carried you as an eagle carries her young on her wings, and brought you here to me. Now if you will obey me and keep my covenant, you will be my own people" (Ex 19:4–5). The prophets, with increasing clarity and vigor, call Israel to extend that covenant, eventually written on hearts, to all peoples; and Jesus invites all people into a new covenant written in his blood.

Although Christians have continued to spill blood and shatter that covenant by the demon nationalism, the core of biblical faith is that all people are one "in Christ." "There are no more distinctions between Jew and Greek, slave and free, male and female, but all of you are one in Christ Jesus" (Gal 3:28). "Christ himself has made our reconciliation" (Eph 2:14). Therefore, the Spirit of God who makes us one calls us beyond "hatred and fighting, jealousy and anger, constant effort to get the best for yourself, complaints and criticisms, the feeling that everyone else is wrong except those in your own little group" (Gal 5:20).

In our times Paul VI has called us to move beyond the nationalism of "our own little group": "The principal fact that we must all recognize is that the social question has become worldwide."[12] The Gospel challenge is to broaden our vision beyond Church and nation and extend the covenant to all our brothers and sisters in the Kingdom of God.

John Coleman suggests that Catholicism has within itself some special gifts of universality which might help our nation deal more effectively with the challenges of interdependence.

The greatest possible strength of Catholicism in social ethics consists in its potential for generating primordial loyalties to a community which transcends the na-

tion, to weave into Catholic life a texture of deep
symbols which could evoke for Catholics a sense that
they are citizens and members of a community of
worldwide dimensions.[13]

Within Catholicism there are traditions of liturgy, literature, transnational unity with a people and a Pope which give
expression to a covenant crossing national boundaries. If Catholics were to live that vision, they might serve as a "committee on
humankind."

Coleman also suggests that in our particular historical moment in America the Catholic Church has unique gifts which
might move us beyond nationalism. Those gifts are Catholic ethnic groups of Hispanics, Cubans, Haitians, Vietnamese, many of
them refugees, poor and lower middle-class. These people might
not only keep the Catholic social conscience alive to the poverty
of our brothers and sisters in this country but also bond us to
their brothers and sisters throughout the world, in a more ex-
pansive covenant. Unlike the European Church which lost the
working class and the poor, American Catholics who remain
sensitive to linking all classes within their own Church might
make a unique contribution to the exorcising of nationalism.
That might refurbish the Statue of Liberty to welcome "all your
tired, your poor, your huddled masses yearning to be free" and
extend a covenant of justice not only to our shores but to all
shores. As James Joyce said, it has always been catholic to proclaim, "Here comes everybody!" In this context conversion has
enormous implications for the future of humankind. It is inher-
ently political and social; it deals with the *polis*, Joyce's everybody.

From Doomsday Fatalism to Liberating Hope

I sometimes wish that the Book of Revelation had never
been written. In these days of nuclear terror it offers a fertile
field for true believers in Apocalypse Now to portray in vivid
detail the last days of the great planet earth. The world has

"ended" before. In those dark days when the Roman Empire collapsed and with it the Roman faith in law and the Greek faith in reason, all sorts of weird gnostic religions flourished with grand stories of wars among the gods, human fate determined by the stars, and wondrous revelations about the end of time. In our times, filled with talk of doomsday and flirtation with astrology charts and ouija boards which determine our fate, gnostic religions should sound familiar.

I don't mean to take our terror lightly. Some research indicates that many people, especially young people, believe that nuclear holocaust is inevitable. Therefore, no long-term commitments; back to Ecclesiastes—eat, drink and be merry for tomorrow you may die. The suicide rate among children has increased three hundred percent in the past few years. That leaves out the "walking dead" who feel trapped in their jobs, with weary fatigue about life, stumbling around from 9 to 5 and then from 5 to 9 with glazed resignation. Walter Brueggemann remarks that Israelites tend to complain rather than lament. The Exodus was a kind of primal scream against slavery, a cry against fatalism. The great song of Moses is the most eloquent, liberating song of Israel; and the prophets forever remember the Exodus and keep Israel singing. But Brueggemann also notes, "If the lack of singing is an index of exile, then we are in it, for we are a people who scarcely sing."[14]

Earlier I mentioned my concern that reflection on the social dimensions of conversion might simply leave us with guilt, with fatalism about issues so immense that we feel powerless to confront them. That is why I close these reflections with some words about hope.

Hope also has a social twist. The Act of Hope that my generation learned in elementary school was very private. We hoped for "the pardon of my sins, the help of Thy grace, and life everlasting through the merits of Jesus Christ, my Lord and Redeemer." Biblical hope is cosmic.

> Then I saw a new heaven and a new earth. . . . I saw the
> holy city, and the new Jerusalem, coming down from

God out of heaven, as beautiful as a bride all dressed
for her husband. Then I heard a loud voice call from
the throne, "You see this city? Here God lives among
people. He will make his home among them; they shall
be his people, and he will be their God; his name is
God-with-them. He will wipe away all tears from their
eyes; there will be no more death, and no more mourn-
ing or sadness. The world of the past is gone" (Rev
21:1–4).

The good news is that the future is now—not the future of
doomsday but our resurrection in Jesus begins now. We are a
graced people now. Not Apocalypse Now but Resurrection
Now. The demons are more than private sins, but the Holy
Spirit also is no private possession. The Spirit possesses us now,
as a people. We are recreated in God's image by that Spirit, and
nothing is more important than to know the kind of God in
whose image we are created. Ours is a God of freedom, of exodus, of justice, of liberation. Ours is a God who makes all things
new. In the Spirit of that God, we make all things new. Therefore, we hope.

Brueggemann points out that ours are not the first barren
times.

Barrenness is a proper theme among us for it is more
than television, which is a wasteland. Our society is
filled with eunuchs of both sexes whose manhood and
womanhood are taken by the corporation. There is no
hope, no future, and therefore no children. There is
not enough energy to bear or beget, and who wants to
birth new children for Babylon? Our history always
begins with the barren, with Sarah (Gen. 11:30), with
Rebekah (Gen. 25:21), with Rachel (Gen. 29:31), and
with Elizabeth (Luke 1:7). Among those, always as good
as dead (Heb. 11:12), the wondrous gift is given. . . . It is
often news—good news, doxology—which brings the
new energy to effect and the new future to birth.[15]

The prophets bring that good news:

Sing, O barren one, who did not bear;
   break forth into singing and cry aloud,
   you who have not been in labor!
For the children of the desolate one will be more
   than the children of her that is married, says the Lord
   (Is 54:1).

Our times cry for prophets to exorcise the demons of consumerism, privatism, nationalism, fatalism. More critically, our
times call for prophets to paint before us images of hope, images
of who we can be as a people. We have the image. We have him
who revealed to us that *we are the images*. He is "the image of the
invisible God" (Col 1:15), the gift of God, on mission from the
Father, our new covenant, our liberating hope. We have seen
him. We have heard the good news. In him we have seen the future:

Something which has existed since the beginning,
that we have heard
and we have seen with our own eyes;
that we have watched
and touched with our hands;
the Word, who is life—
this is our subject.
That life was made visible;
we saw it and we are giving our testimony,
telling you of the eternal life
which was with the Father and has been made visible to us.
What we have seen and heard
we are telling you
so that you too may be in union with us
as we are in union
with the Father
and with his Son Jesus Christ.
We are writing this to you to make our own joy complete
   (1 Jn 1:1–4).

Jesus Christ, leading us in the Spirit into the Kingdom now, is my hope for you, for me, for all of humankind, and even for you, Mrs. Turpin, you old wart hog!

Notes

1. Flannery O'Connor, "Revelation," in *Flannery O'Connor: The Complete Stories.* New York: Farrar, Straus, and Giroux, 1971, p. 508.

2. Karol Cardinal Wojtyla, September, 1976, quoted in *The Wall Street Journal,* November 9, 1978.

3. "Justice in the World," Introduction, *The Pope Speaks* 16 (1972), pp. 377, 381.

4. John Francis Kavanaugh, *Following Christ in a Consumer Society: The Spirituality of Cultural Resistance.* Maryknoll: Orbis Books, 1982, p. 34.

5. Pope John Paul II, Homily at Mass at Yankee Stadium, *Origins* 9, 19 (October 25, 1979), p. 311.

6. The language of this paragraph is partly mine and partly that of Frederick Buechner, *Telling the Truth: The Gospel as Tragedy, Comedy, and Fairy Tale.* New York: Harper and Row, 1977, *passim.*

7. Nathan Mitchell, "Exorcism in the RCIA," *Christian Initiation Resources* I, 3 (1981), p. 163.

8. Buechner, *Telling the Truth,* p. 66.

9. Jim Wallis, *The Call to Conversion: Recovering the Gospel for These Times.* New York: Harper and Row, 1981, p. 34.

10. Robert Bellah, *The Broken Covenant: American Civil Religion in a Time of Trial.* New York: Seabury Press, 1975, p. 14.

11. Bellah, *The Broken Covenant,* p. 1.

12. Paul VI, *Populorum Progressio,* no. 3.

13. John A. Coleman, *An American Strategic Theology.* New York: Paulist Press, 1982, p. 236.

14. Walter Brueggemann, *The Prophetic Imagination.* Philadelphia: The Fortress Press, 1978, p. 72.

15. Brueggemann, *The Prophetic Imagination,* p. 76.

Conversion in the Bible

Michael Brennan Dick

Introduction

The idea of "conversion" forms a bright trajectory through both Testaments of the Bible. To a considerable degree the entire dynamic of God's word in its human encounter—from the word that created to the Word made flesh—can be captured by the notion of conversion. Here God's powerful summons to intimacy confronts the mystery of human free will. Much of the Jewish Scriptures revolves around the Moses-Sinai covenant which not only initiated Israel's alliance with Yahweh but also underscored Israel's responsibilities towards that covenant. The Sinai covenant, like the contemporary treaties between a sovereign and his vassal upon which it was modeled, was contingent upon the vassal's faithfulness. Whenever Israel strayed from its treaty with Yahweh, the prophets would summon the people to return ("convert"). And so conversion stresses the persistent need of the nation to examine its stance and to return to its foundation. In the Christian Scriptures the Baptist's cry to convert both inaugurates the new era and summarizes the mission of Jesus (Lk 5:32).

Despite the importance of conversion for both Jewish and Christian Scriptures the Bible does not have a distinct, focused doctrine of conversion. We must be wary of imposing on the text doctrinal interests of a later era; and so problems such as the possibility of a "second conversion" for the most part either are not considered or are not developed systematically. Nevertheless, certain characteristics do emerge, which are common to many of the different biblical views of conversion.

(1) First of all, conversion generally involves (re-)establishing a personal relationship with God. Even when this relation is formulated within the framework of a covenant, it is decidedly personal. For example, in the prophets of Israel the Hebrew word "convert" (*shub*) is most often accompanied by the prepositional phrase with the personal object "to Yahweh" (Am 4:6ff): the return is a realignment of loyalty between persons.

(2) Biblical conversion embraces all human faculties: rational, volitional, and affective. For Jeremiah (24:7), Ezekiel (18:30–31), and Psalm 51:9–12 this new relationship to God (Jeremiah's and Ezekiel's new covenant) would only be possible if humans were granted both a new spirit and a new heart, the Hebrew organ of intelligence. But conversion particularly appeals to the will and the emotional faculty. Even though conversion is a gift offered by God, it remains open to human free will. Furthermore, conversion is more than a "change of mind"; it is an affective realignment which Hosea appropriately likened to the reconciliation of a husband with his faithless wife.

(3) Conversion represents a mysterious interplay ("synergism") between the human and divine. The challenge to convert is totally a divine gift: "Lead us back to you, O Lord, that we might be restored; give us anew such days as we had of old" (Lam 5:21 NAB). Yet the response is also wholly human. Here we enter that enigmatic arena of grace and nature which penetrates to the very heart of the incarnation and God's plan.

(4) This summons is also communal: the conversion imperative is normally plural and is addressed to the people of Israel and to the Church. The individual is summoned back into the people created by the Sinai covenant and into the *ecclesia* of the new covenant.

(5) Throughout the Bible conversion is inescapably moral. The truly converted demonstrate their new relationship by their changed conduct. Turning toward God is simultaneously a turning away from sin. This ethical dimension is particularly stressed in Ezekiel ("turn from your evil way") and in Luke.

(6) Both the Jewish and Christian Scriptures generally describe conversion as an ongoing *process* and not as an *event*. They symbolize this by their use of the metaphor of the "journey." And so conversion is often associated with the arduous trek of the Israelities from bondage in Egypt to a new relationship with Yahweh on Sinai (the exodus). Luke refers to it as a "road." The Easter vigil which ideally seals the conversion of the adult Christian with baptism is rooted in exodus symbolism. Not surprisingly the RCIA frequently describes Christian conversion as a journey.

Jeremiah depicts conversion as an ongoing possibility which could happen in both directions: we could just as easily turn *from* Yahweh as *toward* him (Jer 8:4–5). This realignment was not once and for all; Jeremiah portrayed Judah as a constantly "turning people" (Jer 3:22) who had always to face the possibility of rejecting God and of being summoned to return. Indeed the entire Jewish Scripture could be conceived as the journey of Israel toward and away from Yahweh. Still the prophets made clear that God's patience was not unlimited: he would not permit his call to be cheapened. Even Hosea who most clearly saw this cycle warned that Yahweh would not allow new covenant and new exodus endlessly to follow upon the sin of Israel.

The Bible prefers verbs to nouns when it refers to conversion. Both the Hebrew Bible and the New Testament show a clear preference for such verbs as Hebrew *shub* ("return") and Greek *metanoeo* ("convert") over their noun counterparts. Conversion is then mostly an activity and not a state or event. Only when conversion appears in an eschatological context—when the sinner is faced with the final judgment—does it become a one time, decisive act with no second opportunity.

(7) In both the Jewish and Christian Scriptures conversion is often associated with symbolic acts. The prophet Joel describes a repentance ceremony (1:13–14; 2:12–17) accompanied by community prayer and fasting in the temple. Psalm 51 associates repentance with sprinkling with water (51:4, 9), and in the Christian Scriptures repentance is linked with baptism of water.

Methodology

In this article I shall focus on those parts of the Bible which emphasize conversion: Jeremiah, Luke, John, and Paul. I prefer to approach each book's view on conversion by studying a few representative passages. Although this method has the obvious disadvantage of appearing more minute and detailed than expected in a general article, it carries the advantage of opening up to the reader the nature of the evidence that is available. If the reader will kindly suffer through a few Greek and Hebrew transliterations (always with translations!), he or she should achieve a sense of the actual biblical text—including its ambiguity. I shall always relate the particular passage being considered to the broader issue. All biblical translations are by the author unless marked NAB (New American Bible).

Conversion in the Old Testament

Almost the entire Jewish Scripture can be oriented around three centers: the Moses-Sinai covenant, the Davidic covenant, and the Zion tradition. The first of these was patterned after ancient Near Eastern treaties according to which Israel's relationship to Yahweh was portrayed as that of vassal to sovereign. Yahweh would protect Israel only *as long as* and *if* Israel, the vassal, would honor the stipulations of the treaty (covenant). The main demand was that Israel recognize Yahweh alone as her Lord (see Ex 20:3). Should Israel falter in her allegiance, then the treaty would be nullified and the curses such as preserved in Deuteronomy 28 would become effective. The use of this international legal metaphor to describe Israel's relationship to Yahweh did not exclude emotional ties, for even in these ancient treaties the rapport of vassal to sovereign was described in terms of "love" and "knowledge" (cf. Hos 6:6). The treaty partners attempted to elevate their association to a personal level.

The Davidic covenant (see 2 Sam 1 and Ps 89) was Yahweh's one-sided promise to stand by David and his family: a member of David's family would rule over Jerusalem forever *no matter what* (cf. Ps 89:31–38). Unlike the Sinai covenant, the Davidic covenant was not reciprocal; Yahweh bound only himself to deliver on his promise; no stipulations such as the decalogue were imposed on David's family. This type of covenant was modeled after the ancient Near Eastern royal grant in which a monarch rewarded a subject with a gift; only the sovereign was bound in this type covenant.

The Zion tradition was also perceived as a one-sided relationship between Jerusalem and Yahweh. Every oriental deity was linked with a mountain, e.g., Baal with Mount Zaphon. Yahweh was bound in a special way to the temple on Mount Zion which was then described in mythic terms as the center of the universe, the source of fertilizing streams of water, the highest mountain, etc. (cf. Pss 46 and 48). A popular corollary of this belief was that Yahweh's presence on Zion guaranteed the inviolability of the Davidic capital from her enemies.

The emphasis in the Zion tradition and in the Davidic covenant on what Yahweh promised Israel was in tension with the Mosaic religion which stressed Israel's obligations toward Yahweh. In fact much of the theology of the Hebrew Scripture can be understood as a struggle among these three religious concepts. Conversion plays no role in the Davidic covenant and the Zion tradition, for these two do not underscore the people's response to God's pledge. Israel is not expected to "turn toward" Yahweh and accept them. The emphasis in their exaggerated form is more on God's responsibility. Conversion is related to the Sinai covenant which requires Israel constantly to assess her relation to her sovereign. The summons to conversion is usually encountered in those places in which the Mosaic religion is being asserted against the dangers of "easy grace" inherent in the other two traditions; its call is especially heard among the prophets who were special guardians of the Mosaic covenant.

Conversion and Israel's Roots

According to one theory about the origins of Israel, the people owed their very existence to conversion. George E. Mendenhall and Norman K. Gottwald have advanced similar theses about Israel's entrance into and "conquest" of the promised land of Canaan. They suggest that there was no invasion of united Israelite tribes from across the Jordan River. Instead they theorize that there was an internal peasant revolt against the oppressive Late Bronze Age city states. (In fact such an upheaval is earlier documented in the Amarna Correspondence between Palestine and Egypt.) This guerrilla movement was unified by the entrance into the mountain areas of a small group of newcomers from Egypt who had undergone a religious transformation in the Sinai desert. The newcomers had thrown off bondage in Egypt and now patterned their relation to God after a treaty in which Yahweh replaced the earthly sovereign. It was a religion of profound liberation! Such a novel view of religion was immediately relevant to the countless disorganized rebel bands in the mountains of Palestine. They *converted* to the Sinai religion. The Sinai covenant became the symbol by which their solidarity was effected; only later was this unity expressed according to the tradition of twelve tribes being the offspring of their common father Jacob. Joshua 24 is an example of such a conversion ceremony by which the people are required to turn from the gods of their fathers toward the God of Sinai. If this hypothesis is accepted, then Israel owed its very existence to conversion. Conversion rather than blood was the process by which they became the people of Yahweh.

Regardless of which view the reader accepts for the creation of Israel, Israel before the exile in 587 generally remained completely disinterested in bringing outsiders into its religion. (Indeed this disinterest is often regarded as evidence against the theories of Mendenhall and Gottwald with their theorized mass conversion of outsiders.) The alien was not assimilated into Israel by conversion, but only by generations of intermarriage. "Conversion" then normally refers to the stance of the Israelite regarding the foundational Mosaic covenant. Since this agreement was by its very nature contingent upon the faithfulness of the people, it was important that Israel continually maintain her relationship with Yahweh or else risk severing her covenantal ties with God. The prophets of Israel were the watchmen of Israel; for over five hundred years the role of the majority of the prophets was either to demand that Israel turn back to the God of Sinai or else to announce the imposition of the curses of the broken covenant.

A major difficulty in reading the prophets is knowing precisely what we are reading. Most prophetic books underwent centuries of editing and reapplication to new crises. For example, when we study Jeremiah and conversion, are we interested in arriving at the view of the original Jeremiah, or of a later stage of editing over the next five hundred years? In my presentation I am more concerned with the overall view of the finished canonical book than with any of its theoretical earlier stages. This distinction is theologically important. Jeremiah himself might have begun his career as prophet with a confidence in the people's willingness to convert, and over the years of his career he might have arrived at the notion that conversion was in fact impossible. However, I am not interested in reconstructing a chronology of Jeremiah's preaching; the finished book, now embracing all stages of his theology as well as centuries of reuse in the community, preserves a tension and ambiguity which speaks God's word to the Church and Synagogue.

To Amos, conversion had not taken place despite countless warnings from Yahweh (Am 4:6ff): "And still you did not turn back to me." Like all the prophets, Amos regarded conversion as personal ("... to me") and a communal responsibility ("you" plural). Therefore Yahweh's punishment would be devastating (Am 9:1–4). However, Amos 5:4 and 5:14–15 seem to offer another chance for repentance: seek God, do good, and *perhaps* Yahweh will have pity on the remnant of Jacob. These verses were probably written by a later editor who was familiar with the theology of the Book of Deuteronomy. However, their inclusion within the otherwise dim prophecies of Amos freezes the book in a final (and canonical) form in which conversion is an open possibility. The threatening word "remnant" (5:15) cautions us that conversion does not preclude punishment.

Hosea, the northern prophet who lived a few years later, boldly likened the relation of vassal/sovereign to husband/wife. Israel (the wife) had been unfaithful (adulterous) to Yahweh (her husband). Unfaithfulness in marriage like irresponsibility in covenant leads to breakup (Hos 1:8). Punishment is inevitable! Cultic attempts to return to Yahweh without re-examining Israel's basic covenant would fail (6:1–7); Yahweh wanted conversion rooted in covenant faithfulness (n.b. covenantal language in v. 6: "love," "knowledge"). According to the law code later written in Deuteronomy 24:1–4, a divorced wife who had remarried could not be received back by her first husband. In human terms, Israel could never again hope for intimacy with her God. But Yahweh is not human!

> I will not give vent to my blazing anger, I will not destroy Ephraim again; for I am God and not man (11:9, NAB).

Hosea speaks of a recapitulation of Israel's historical cycle: there will be as punishment a new slavery in "Egypt" (11:5), but this will be followed by a return to Yahweh (2:9) and a new covenant (2:20ff); finally there will be a return to the land from which they had been exiled.

The contemporary prophet Isaiah of Jerusalem was concerned especially with the Davidic covenant (cf. Is 7:1—9:6) and the Zion tradition, both of which were peculiar to his capital city. Although he does not mention Moses or Sinai in the first thirty-nine chapters attributed to him, he is still heavily influenced by the theology of the Sinai covenant and its demands for conversion. For example, Isaiah 1:2ff follows the literary style of the covenant lawsuit such as found in Micah 6 and Psalm 50. The entire rationale for the lawsuit is that the vassal has violated his treaty and is being held legally accountable by his sovereign; and so Isaiah 1 presupposes the Mosaic covenant. We also find the concomitant theology of conversion in Isaiah.

Isaiah's son Shear-jashub (Is 7:3) bore a name symbolic of his father's views about conversion. The name has three meanings: (1) "only a remnant will return (from exile)"; (2) "a (surviving) remnant will return"; (3) "a remnant will return to Yahweh." The first rendition is an oracle of judgment: for Judah's lack of faith, she will be so punished that only a small portion will survive (cf. 10:22). The second emphasizes the more hopeful note that destruction is not Yahweh's last word; the nation will survive (cf. 10:20). The third understanding of the boy's name prophesies that after a purifying punishment (cf. 1:25–26) the nation will "convert" to the Holy One of Israel (10:21).

Isaiah sees punishment as inevitable for this people (Is 6:9–13); however, the catastrophes to come are pedagogic; they serve to prepare Judah for a "return" to true faithfulness, which for Isaiah is reliance on Yahweh rather than on human arrogance and feelings of self-sufficiency.

> For thus says the Lord Yahweh the Holy One of Israel:
> "In returning and quiet you would be saved, in peace
> and trust would be your strength; but you were unwill-
> ing" (Is 30:15).

A century after Isaiah (ca. 622) Judah was undergoing a religious crisis. Even the Davidic king had to turn to the Mosaic tradition to rejuvenate the nation. Two forces were responsible for reforming Judah, and both of them (the Deuteronomic movement and Jeremiah) looked to the Sinai covenant in order to return the nation to its roots. For Jeremiah conversion embodies the very heart of his message to Jerusalem. Almost a half of all instances of "convert" (*shub*) in the covenantal sense appear in the Book of Jeremiah. For the first time the word "return" can appear without the prepositional phrase "to Yahweh," and by itself refer unambiguously to religious conversion. The Book of Jeremiah even defines the task of the prophet in terms of "bringing" the people back (23:22).

Jeremiah's theology of conversion emerges in the puns on the different cognates and meanings of *shub* found in 8:4–5:

> Do people fall and not rise up again? Does any one turn
> (away) (*yashub*) and not turn (back to God) (*yashub*)?

> Why is this people of Jerusalem turned away (*shobebah*)
> in eternal turning (*meshubah*)? They hold onto deceit,
> but refuse to repent (*shub*).

The prophet stresses that "turning" goes both ways: one can turn away from God as well as toward him. Herein lies both the tragedy of Judah as well as the key to her salvation. Anytime somebody falls down, he or she can always rise up again. *Shub* now means "to change one's covenantal loyalty." If fickle Judah can turn away from her covenantal responsibilities, this same ability to realign herself guarantees her capacity to re-turn to Yahweh.

Jeremiah's poem in 3:1—4:2 exploits this view of conversion. Jeremiah 3:1–5 recalls the imagery of Hosea: an unfaithful wife once divorced and remarried cannot legally (Dt 24:1ff) return to her original husband. Judah has violated the Sinai covenant (cf. 11:10); humanly speaking, she cannot return to her God. Yet God is not human! In vv. 12b–14 Yahweh begs this "turnable" people to return to him; covenantal intimacy is not precluded. The personal level of this relationship is clear in Yahweh's use of the word "sons" in vv. 14 and 19. In the latter verse (v. 19) God expresses the poignant hope that they will not turn away from him again.

The conditions for Judah's return are stipulated in 4:1: the summons to repent might originate with Yahweh, but the people must answer with deeds and reject idolatry. Later additions to the book reinforce this idea that a turning toward God must be marked by a turning away from evil behavior (18:11; 25:5; 26:3; 35:15). (This latter emphasis is particularly strong in Ezekiel.)

Conversion then demands a total personal realignment of loyalty; this return to the covenant embraces the internal faculties (Hebrew "heart") as well as external conduct. The following Deuteronomic phrase which is found in the Book of Jeremiah envisions this complete reversal:

> I will give them a heart with which to understand that
> I am Yahweh. They shall be my people and I shall be

their God, for they will return to me with their whole heart (24:7).

The "heart" here encompasses total consent; human ability to make such a consent is itself God's gift. According to Jeremiah, conversion shall have to be the work of Yahweh, for the people have shown an almost essential inability to convert:

Can the Ethiopian change his skin? The leopard his spots? As easily would you be able to do good, accustomed to evil as you are (13:23).

Judah's refusal to turn back to her sovereign Yahweh has frustrated Yahweh's intentions. The story of the potter in chapter 18 suggests that the potter may be forced by the quality of clay he is working on to change his plans (v. 4). In God's explanation to Jeremiah (vv. 7–10) he warns that Judah's refusal to convert will cause Yahweh to change his good intent. Verse 11 might still hold open the possibility of conversion and the avoidance of God's judgment, but the next verse notes their refusal. The rest of the chapter (vv. 13–17) highlights Judah's ingratitude and her subsequent punishment. Apostasy (likewise called *shub* in Jeremiah) merits destruction (see chapter 5)! God's patience is not unlimited.

However, like Hosea, Jeremiah does not see punishment as terminal (cf. 5:18). The prophet's task was not only to "tear down" and "uproot," but also "to build" and "to plant" (1:10; 31:28). Yahweh himself will intervene after judgment to restore (*shub*) the people (32:37). *Shub* here means not only a return from exile but a spiritual return from their earlier apostasy. This new rapport is described as a new covenant (31:31).

You chastised me, and I am chastened; I was an untamed calf. If you allow me, I will return, for you are Yahweh, my God. I turn in repentance; I have come to myself, I strike my breast; I blush with shame, I bear the disgrace of my youth (31:18–19).

Luke and the Synoptic Gospels

In Matthew (3:2ff), Mark (1:4), and Luke (3:7), John the Baptist proclaims conversion (*metanoia*). In the first two Gospels the cry is urgently eschatological: "Convert for the end is at hand!" Matthew calls for a complete rupture with the sinner's past life and a return to God. This is the sinner's *last* opportunity: "Even now the axe is laid to the root of the tree" (Mt 3:10, NAB). In Matthew and Mark the imperative "Reform your lives!" is based on the indicative "The reign of God is at hand" (Mt 4:17//Mk 1:15). Although John the Baptist is portrayed in continuity with the prophets of the Old Testament, the tone is urgently eschatological. This change is offered once; the "appointed time" has arrived (Mk 1:15); it is a final opportunity for Jews (Mt 3:7ff) as well as Gentiles (Lk 3:14).

Conversion should also exhibit itself in the conduct of the believer: "Do therefore fruit worthy of conversion" (Mt 3:8). "Fruit" is a term frequently used in apocalyptic literature (Mt 7:19; 12:33; Lk 6:43–44). Matthew's "fruit" (n.b. the singular) represents a general comportment and fundamentally changed attitude. Such a conversion leads to the forgiveness of sins, an early Christian belief which is not found in the earlier Greek Old Testament (Acts 2:38; 5:31; 10:43; Eph 1:7; Col 1:14).

Like every prophet before him, John the Baptist accompanies his announcement with a symbolic act, baptism with water. Whoever undergoes baptism with water will avoid the devastating baptism of the storm and of fire when the great harvest is gathered in.

Conversion (*metanoia*) assumes particular significance in Luke's Gospel. The verb "convert" is used sixteen times in the Synoptic Gospels, nine times in Luke; the noun appears eight times, five in Luke. However, more significantly still, out of these fourteen times that the noun and verb are used, only four of them are in places common to the synoptic tradition. That is, ten of the uses are unique to Luke's Gospel. According to Luke, conversion is an essential term for defining the mission of Jesus: "I have not come to invite the self-righteous to conversion but

sinners" (Lk 5:32). In the parallel accounts in Matthew 9:13 and
Mark 2:17, we do not find the phrase "to conversion," which is
peculiar to Luke's understanding of the purpose of Jesus.

Luke's portrayal of the Baptist clearly demonstrates his particular view of conversion. Only Luke has the passage detailing
the ethics of the Baptist (3:10–14). Here John counsels no disrup-
tion of the social order, the sharing of necessities, and content-
ment. This is hardly an ethics of an imminent end! In Luke's
parallel to Matthew 3:8, the evangelist orders the convert to perform the *fruits* of conversion (n.b. the plural instead of Matthew's singular). Luke refers to an entire series of moral acts by
which the sinner should prove the genuineness of his or her
conversion. Luke de-emphasizes the eschatological urgency
found in Matthew and Mark and stresses the ethical aspects of
conversion.

Were this use of the plural rather than the singular the only
evidence, our case for a new understanding of conversion in
Luke would be quite slim, but there is a consistent pattern. First
of all, Luke has omitted some eschatological passages found in
Matthew (4:17) and Mark (1:15) which place conversion in the
context of the final days. Secondly, Luke frequently "ethicizes"
conversion by linking it with the term "sinners."

Luke's version of the call of Levi (5:27–32), which we have
already used to show how the evangelist defines the mission of
Jesus, serves as a Lukan paradigm for his understanding of conversion. Levi's invitation to follow Jesus leads to the tax collec-
tor's "leaving everything" (5:28), a comment found only in Luke
which represents a Lukan ethical ideal (cf. Acts 2:44ff). Luke
then mentions that Levi threw Jesus a banquet (v. 29)—a logical
contradiction for a recently impoverished sinner but a theological symbol mentioned only in Luke. The banquet represents the
ecclesial gathering; Luke's invitation is no longer to the reign of
God, but to the Church.

Years ago H. Conzelmann demonstrated that Luke wrote to
prepare his community for a longer wait, for a future that allowed for an indefinite existence before judgment. The imminent reign of God has been replaced by Christ, the Spirit, and

the Christian ethic, which Luke calls a "journey." The Church is the indefinite period of grace which opens up the possibility of conversion to all thanks to the apostolic preaching. John the Baptist's final call to conversion was once and for all; Luke exhorts sinners to a repentance which is individual and partial (5:32; 15:7, 10; 17:3–4; 24:27). Although certain passages in Luke have even suggested the possibility of a "second conversion" after a relapse (cf. Simon Magus in Acts 8:22), this is probably to impose a precision on the text which Luke had not intended.

Conversion in St. John's Gospel

Although John avoids the word for conversion which the Synoptics prefer, conversion still plays a major role in his Gospel. John used the word "believe" to define the transition into union with the Lord. This verb is used ninety-eight times in John as opposed to thirty-four times in all of the other Gospels. In fact John defines the entire purpose of his gospel in terms of belief.

> Jesus performed many other signs as well—signs not recorded here—in the presence of his disciples. But these have been recorded to help you believe that Jesus is the Messiah, the Son of God, so that through this faith you may have life in his name (Jn 20:30–31, NAB).

According to St. John conversion to life in the Lord is *not* humanly possible (6:65). The Nicodemus episode in 3:1–21 illustrates this. First of all, the word "to be able" is important in the passage (vv. 2, 3, 4 [twice], 5, 9). Humanly speaking, belief is impossible: "No one can see the reign of God without being born from above" (v. 3). This is further strengthened in the next episode in the chapter (v. 27). John also stresses the contrast between the *human* ("flesh") and the *heavenly* ("spirit" and "from above"). Flesh in John does not carry the Pauline connotation of sinfulness; rather it denotes the human as opposed to the divine power and life at work in the world as spirit. Only the spirit can beget belief. This role of the spirit as begetter of life also links faith with Jesus' death and resurrection (7:39; 19:30, 34–35).

Although there are amazing similarities between John and the writings of the monks at Qumran on the Dead Sea (e.g., contrast between light and darkness), there is a significant difference in John's insistence on faith being a free choice. There is no trace of Qumran's determinism. Conversion to Jesus may be begotten from above, but it is also a human decision. Jesus provokes the believer to this choice which is cleverly described in John by the Greek verb *krinein* which means both "to judge" and "to condemn" (cf. 12:46–48). The believer who will not make the decision has already judged himself! This explains John's use of testimony and signs; he is trying to appeal to reason to aid in this choice. John 12:46–48 makes it clear that this option for or against is an eschatological decision ("on the last day"). John also describes Jesus as the light who highlights the choice which we are summoned to make (3:19–21).

The choice made by the believer reflects itself in his or her deeds (3:19–21). The evil spoken of in v. 20 is not merely *a* sin; rather Jesus is speaking here of one who practices radical evil. According to John, our conversion must be maintained even in the face of disbelief in the community (John's Gospel) and in the face of heresy (the Epistles, e.g. 1 Jn 2:18f; 4:1–6). Scandal is another threat to the believer (6:60f, 66). The believer must expect a continual series of crises which will challenge his or her belief (6:66–68). This is especially true of the passion of Jesus which seriously threatened the relation of the disciples to Jesus (13:19; 14:1, 29; 16:13).

John's emphasis on sacramentalism relates conversion to baptism more clearly than in any other Christian writing. The baptismal interpretation of the Nicodemus passage is quite early. The story of the cure of the man born blind (Jn 9) also connects conversion with baptism. The blind man is cured by immersion in a pool called Siloam, which John translates "one who has been sent." "The one who has been sent" is a phrase frequently used to describe Jesus himself (3:17, 34; 5:36, 38). The emphasis in this miracle story about the man being *born* blind and being *born* in sin also suggests the baptismal language of (re-) birth.

Faith in the Fourth Gospel is a personal commitment to Jesus, not merely a "belief that." In 1:11 conversion is referred to as "receiving" Jesus. In general John prefers the more personal form of expression, "belief in," to denote this new relationship. John also uses the language of discipleship—to follow Jesus. Conversion as a journey—a motif used in the RCIA—also finds support in this Gospel. John frequently refers to conversion as "coming to Jesus" (6:35); this is especially evident in passages describing the call of the first disciples (1:40, 47f; cf. 3:2, 26;; 4:30).

St. John's view of faith is decidedly ecclesial; this is clear in his symbolism of the vine (15) and of the flock (10). Notice that in the call of the disciples almost every disciple is brought to Jesus by another (1:35–51; people of Shechem 4:29f, 39f); the summons to conversion is mediated by the community. After the time of Jesus the invitation to faith comes through apostolic testimony: "I do not pray for them alone. I pray also for those who will believe in me through *their* word . . ." (17:20). John is concerned that the early Church of his day feel an unbroken link with its Lord—especially now that the last of the original followers of Jesus have died. This is probably the intent of Jesus' prayer for unity (17:22): "That all might be one, as we are one." Jesus prays that the eras of Jesus, of the first converts, and of the Church of John's time might all be one. Jesus imposes on the community the commandment of love which is to unite the church of believers (15:9, 12).

The RCIA recognizes a growth and development within the conversion process; this approach also finds support in John. The faith of the disciples was gradual (2:22, 12:16). The Holy Spirit plays a decisive role in the progression of this faith (14:26; 16:13). Johannine faith, then, has degrees. It can be of lesser degree both because of the nature of the confession (9:22; 14:22; 19:38) or because of the motive (4:48). This progression is skillfully conveyed in the story about the healing of the blind man (chapter 9). By degrees the blind man whose sight was restored first confesses Jesus as a prophet (v. 17), then addresses Jesus as "sir" (v. 36); finally he confesses Jesus as the Lord of worship (v. 38).

Conversion in the Epistles of St. Paul

The usual terms for conversion in the Synoptics were *metanoeo* and *metanoia*, which Paul rarely uses and even then not uniformly. He employs the Greek word *epistrepho* ("to turn to") both in a neutral sense (cf. Gal 4:9) and predominantly in passages which either cite the Septuagint (2 Cor 3:16) or preserve traditional creedal statements (1 Thess 1:9–10). In short, Paul was not content merely to develop the theology of conversion witnessed in the first three gospels; he has created his own vocabulary to express his own particular view.

I shall first treat several passages which reflect the more traditional terminology, and then I shall present the view(s) of conversion which are more peculiar to Paul.

(A) Metanoeo/Metanoia in Paul
Romans 2:4

This is one of the few passages where Paul uses the term *metanoia*. The entire passage (1:18—2:29) is a speech addressed to a fictitious adversary (2:1) who probably represents the Jewish people. The listener agrees with Paul's condemnation of Israel's enemies, but now Paul uses this as the basis for calling Israel to repentance. He suggests that the Jews display a misguided confidence in their special status; they exhibit a "hardened and unrepentant heart" (2:5). They have forgotten that the patience of God is meant to afford them an opportunity for conversion (*metanoia*), which will shelter them from the eschatological day of wrath spoken of in 2:5. This passage is full of irony, for it echoes Wisdom 11:23–24 which also speaks of God "leading" people to conversion; but unlike Romans, Wisdom speaks of the Gentiles being brought to repentance by God. Paul then suggests that the Jews have changed places with the Gentiles!

2 Corinthians 7:9-12

This passage extends from 7:5 to 7:13 (or 7:16). Verses 9-12 establish the difference between conversion and mere emotional upheaval. Grief endured "in God's way" leads to conversion which in turn effects salvation, while human regret borne "in the world's way" leads to death. (Also see 2 Cor 7:8.)

2 Corinthians 12:21

This is the only occurrence of the verb *metanoeo* in Paul. This section is part of a larger passage (12:19—13:10) which reflects Paul's anxiety over the relapses of so many in the Corinthian church. Many have succumbed to libertinism and so their repentance from previous sins is not yet complete. The verb "to sin before" is in the perfect tense whereas "to repent" is aorist. This use of different tenses suggests that conversion is not merely a once and for all prerequisite for entrance into the community but a persistent attitude by which the life of faith is constantly challenged (13:5). The status of this life of faith is clearly revealed in the ethical conduct of the believer. The sins of the past still threaten the Corinthian church (use of perfect tense) and constantly subject it to the conversion imperative (aorist).

(B) Conversion as Transformation

In many exhortative sections in the Epistles, Paul uses the words "form" (*morphe*) and "shape" (*schema*) to describe the conversion "transformation." These words express an anticipation of the end of the time (1 Thess 1:10; 3:12-13) when the Christian will be "shaped to the likeness of his (God's) Son" (Rom 8:29). The appearance of this vocabulary mainly in parenetic passages suggests that in view of the coming judgment the believer should anticipate God's eschatological transformation of his or her life and lead a correspondingly moral life.

Romans 12:2

Do not be shaped to this age, but rather be reformed by
a renewal of the mind so that you can discern the will
of God and what is good, acceptable, and perfect.

Chapter 12 of Romans articulates the moral imperative prepared by the indicative of the earlier eleven chapters: the salvation effected in Jesus Christ places an ethical responsibility
upon the believer. The passive imperative ("be reformed") es-
tablishes that mysterious cooperation between God and the convert. The imperative recognizes the individual's accountability,
while the passive suggests like 2 Corinthians 3:18 that the grace
of this transformation lies outside humankind. Paul's use of the
word "renewal" explains the practical aspects of the believer's
conversion; he or she must effect a complete reversal of values
which encompasses far more than the intellectual faculty. The
renewal of the mind here suggests a reversal of the total life situation.

Philippians 3:21

(Jesus) will reshape our lowly bodies and form them
like his own glorious body by the force which enables
him to subject all things to himself.

Verses 20 and 21 conclude the passage 3:2–21; these two
verses also supply the pivotal point around which the moral im-
peratives found in 3:17 and 4:1 turn (cf. 4:1: "Therefore . . ."). The
vocabulary here unmistakably recalls the Christological hymn
of 2:6–11 where Jesus himself first undertakes this transformation, which then empowers him in the eschaton to transform us.
And so in view of this conversion of our lowly selves we must
now stand firm (4:1)! Clearly, Paul's theology of conversion is
rooted in his Christology.

Galatians 4:19

Galatians 4:8–13 constitutes an emotional plea to avoid the dangers of a relapse into the bondage from which the community had been freed. Here the verb "to form" is used in an implicit exhortation. Although the death of the old self was to take place in baptism (3:27; 2:19–20), this process of rebirth conformed to the Lord is gradual and implies the progressive growth of the ethical life.

(C) Conversion as a New Creation

Using language which recalls Deutero-Isaiah, Paul describes God's transformation of the sinner as a new creation: "Whenever anyone is in Christ there is a new creation; the old order has passed away and the new has begun" (2 Cor 5:17).

> Do not lie to one another, now that you have discarded the old man with his deeds and have put on the new man which is being constantly renewed in the image of his creator; and so there is no longer Greek and Jew, circumcised and uncircumcised, Scythian, freeman, slave; but Christ is all and is in all (Col 3:9–11).

This passage illustrates many characteristics of Paul's view of conversion. First of all, its appearance in the context of a moral imperative once again suggests that Paul bases his ethics in his theology of conversion: our union in Christ has begun a total transformation of our nature which will be completely realized at judgment; this union also confers on us a new ethical responsibility. Colossians 3:9–11 also illustrates the intertwining roles of the human and divine in this conversion. We are summoned to discard the old and put on the new, but the new man has already been renewed by God. Paul has continually insisted on God's power in this transformation (cf. Gal 4:9); conversion is not the same as human perfection. This conversion also is potentially universal and extends beyond Israel.

Paul made clear in Romans 6:3 that this transforming union with Christ is by baptism and the Holy Spirit. Romans also describes conversion as a transfer from slavery to sin to servitude to Jesus (6:20–22), which recalls the metaphor of the sovereign/vassal covenant with which we began this study.

Faith and Sacraments in the Conversion Process

Mark Searle

> *Because our rites are so very simple, so lacking in dramatic effect or gimmicks, and—not the least consideration—because it doesn't cost them anything, it seems utterly incredible that, when people are sent down into the water and washed to the accompaniment of a few words, emerging little or no cleaner than they were before, they nevertheless attain to everlasting life.* [1]

So wrote the North African convert Tertullian in a little booklet on baptism, sometime around the year 200: the rites seem so ordinary, the claims made for them so extraordinary. Tertullian's contemporaries were probably comparing the unprepossessing rituals of the Christians with the powerfully dramatic rites of the pagan mystery religions, but something of the same wonderment bothers people today. There is a widespread sense of unease about making claims about the objectivity of faith or the objective efficacy of sacramental rites which have little or no perceptible relationship to people's actual lives; and yet attempts to make faith and sacraments "relevant" by relating them to experience sometimes seem to do so only at the cost of seeming to water down the Church's traditional teaching. We are caught between what might be called the old objectivism and the new personalism.

This comes to the surface most acutely in the use of the Rite of the Christian Initiation of Adults. Most people working in the catechumenate seem to realize that faith is rather more than the blind acceptance of a set of more or less improbable beliefs, yet the nature of that something more and its relation to the teaching and discipline of the Church is not always grasped with confidence. As a result, many who would do something different if they only knew how end up falling back into "convert instruction." It is easier to teach the "facts of the faith" than to get involved in the unknown territory of what Aidan Kavanagh has called "conversion therapy"; and, after all, "facts" often seem to be what the converts are looking for. Similarly with the liturgical rites of the catechumenate: we are torn between attributing to them some kind of objective, almost "magical" efficacy—with which most would feel uncomfortable—or else reducing them to something we can more easily manage conceptually. So the rites of the RCIA—enrollment and election and scrutinies, especially, but the sacraments of initiation and reception to some degree—tend to become merely ecclesiastical "graduations," marking the converts' progress through the catechumenal program and celebrating what they have learned.

This, then, would seem to be the dilemma: whether to emphasize the objective mystery at the expense of subjective meaning and experience, or to emphasize the "celebration of experience" at the expense of the objective mystery. There would be other ways of posing the problem—such as asking how to relate the doctrines of Catholic Christianity to contemporary experience—but since there seems to be a connection between problems concerning faith and problems concerning rite and sacrament in the catechumenal process, we shall address the issue here theologically in terms of the relationship between faith and sacrament.

I. Faith

1. *Faith as a Human Universal*

Whether "faith" be understood primarily in conceptual terms (that which is believed) or primarily in personalist terms (that by which we believe), it is usually taken for granted that faith is a religious phenomenon, characteristic of religious people. The work of developmental psychologists like Erikson and

Fowler, however, suggests that faith, in Fowler's phrase, is a "human universal." Acording to him, faith designates "a way of leaning into life . . . a way of making sense of one's existence. It denotes a way of giving order and coherence to the force-field of life. It speaks of the investment of life-grounding trust and of life-orienting commitment."[2] Thus understood, faith is the basis of every human life. Fowler traces its development from earliest infancy through childhood and shows that the development of some kind of faith, some sort of making sense of the world, some sense of what, in life, may be trusted and what makes living worthwhile, is integral to the growth and development of every human being. No one lives without faith, without some way of "leaning into life."

Three corollaries follow upon this insight.

First, faith is already present and shaping our lives before we are conscious of it; indeed, so fundamental is it to the very way we exist as persons that it is rarely, if ever, brought to full consciousness. It is only through crisis or confrontation, where our normal way of carrying life on is challenged or breaks down, that we can become aware of the faith we live by. Thus faith, in this sense, is more than what we are able to say about what we believe: it is our deep-seated, pre-reflexive, way of living our life.

Second, while this foundational faith is largely beyond our conscious awareness, it nevertheless underlies all we say and do and manifests itself in our habitual actions and reactions. It is thus something which is embodied in our life and life-style before it "comes to mind." We know who we are when we see what we do; we begin to become aware of the faith we live by when we reflect on how we live. Thus faith is essentially embodied or incarnated in the way we approach life, and our habitual modes of talking and behaving are "outward signs" of this inner reality of faith.

Third, not all faith is religious or, better, theological: i.e., directed to God. While I assume that what Karl Rahner means by the human person's existential orientation to union with God in history is not different from what Fowler describes as the human person's "leaning into life," it is clear that not all leaning is a leaning on God. It is not always God in whom we trust, or who orients our life or receives our commitment. All sorts of other things can usurp that position: self-reliance, the quest for financial security, the American way of life, one's work, personal relationships, ambition, etc. To the degree that these become the objects of our faith, the things that give meaning and direction to human life, they become gods.

What the Scriptures refer to as "false gods," or as "the world," then, would be all the things we rely on, short of the living and true God, to carry out our life-project. It is God's disclosure of himself to us, in the events of our lives and in the Scriptures and sacraments, which enables us to see the faith we live by and to recognize it as an enslavement to false gods. Juan Mateos, on the basis of the Gospels, reduces these gods to three: money (the thirst for wealth), glory (the desire for recognition), and power (the desire to dominate)—all of which constitute ways of trying to secure (or save) our lives.[3] The point to be made here, however, is that people to whom the Gospel is addressed, or people who come to the catechumenate, are not lacking in faith. The challenge is not to give them faith, but to allow their faith(s) to be confronted with the word of God, so that they can recognize the false gods in their lives and submit to the call of the living and true God. This is why the catechumenate has no time limit and why the exorcisms and blessings, the prayer and fasting, the living of a Christian life-style, are all so integral to a process whose culmination is found in the public renunciation of Satan (the "father of lies") and public surrender to God, in Christ and the Church, in the waters of baptism.

2. *Christian Faith*

This approach to faith is clearly consonant with that of Vatican II, which, wishing to counterbalance a too conceptual idea of faith that virtually identified it with belief, returned to Paul's concept of "the obedience of faith" (Rom 16:26). In paragraph 5 of the *Decree on Divine Revelation*, the Council speaks of "the obedience of faith" which "must be given to God who reveals, an obedience by which man entrusts his whole self freely to God, offering 'the full submission of intellect and will to God who reveals,' and freely assenting to the truth revealed by him." The Christian life, then, is a life lived leaning on God who discloses himself as present to save us, not only in the past but in the present, not only in history but in our own lives. It is encounter, initiated by God, to which the only appropriate response is "obedience," "trust," "self-surrender, confidence in God's truthfulness."

In *Paul for a New Day*, Robin Scroggs underlines this Pauline understanding of faith by presenting it as a radically new way of life, in contrast to the ways of the world:

> Faith is not for Paul primarily a series of intellectual, theological propositions, as the term has come to mean in our tradition. Faith is rather that basic stance before the God of grace; it is a quality of existence in the new creation. It is the constant confidence that God has given us our life as sheer gift. It is the courage to remain standing in that place, not to be scared by anxiety, fear, or lack of trust in that old creation based on justification by works. Faith is thus the basic attitude of the believer towards God. And only this stance is eschatological existence. Pauls says it clearly: "Whatever does not come from faith is sin" (Rom 14:23).[4]

Scroggs goes on to point out that, for Paul, obedience does not mean doggedly following a set of commandments, but a willingness to live before God in dependence upon him who continually bestows life as sheer gift. Thus faith requires that we do not turn Christianity into an escape from insecurity, that we live that trust in God consistently, even though such a way of life appears foolish and unwarranted to the "world," i.e. to those whose faith is in themselves or other "gods."

Christian faith is therefore something open-ended, and this in two ways. It is open-ended in the sense that it is a surrender to being led by God into an unknown future; and it is open-ended in that we cannot give our lives totally and entirely over to God in a single momentous decision, but must continually, day by day, take up the opportunities and confront the vicissitudes of life in ways that express and affirm our faith in God.

This double open-endedness of faith might seem to cut us adrift altogether, like some lost astronaut floating off into interminable space, but in fact the opposite is true: it roots us in something much bigger than ourselves.

The faith of the individual Christian is never merely his or her own individual relationship with God. In being called to faith by God, one is called to enter into a pattern of life which is already in place. It is in place in the community of believers, the Church, where the journey into God is a way of life. For this is the essence of the Church: that it is a community of people called by God from the "world," as we have defined it, to live the life of the Spirit of God, the obedience of faith.

For the Church, too, faith is more than doctrine. It is its essential relationship of obedience, submission and trust toward God in the world. This relationship is something which, like the faith of the individual, is largely pre-conscious, is necessarily lived out before it can be articulated, and is open-ended. So the primary "expressions of faith" in the life of the Church are to be sought in those activities which are most typical: the celebration of word and sacrament, the assembling of the people, the care of the poor and the oppressed and the suffering, confrontation with the multifarious forms of false faith and untruth, and the fidelity shown to God despite misunderstanding, opposition and even persecution. Its doctrines are its attempts to reflect upon this life of faith and to articulate its origins, meaning and direction: they are not so much "objects of faith" as ways of entering into the faith-life of the Church, which is faith in God alone.

It is into that faith-life-toward-God that the catechumen is to be initiated, and this must always be kept in mind. The point of whatever instruction may be given in the catechumenate is not to get the catechumens to believe these things—e.g., the assumption of Mary or original sin—but to open them as doors onto the mystery of life toward God. In order to do that, we have to have meditated on the catechism or the feasts and seasons of the liturgical year and discovered how the "mysteries of faith" open onto the life of God, mediating between it and our ordinary life in this visible world.

The key to all this, and what makes our faith in God a properly "Christian" faith, is the faith of Christ himself. If the individual comes to faith through being inserted into the faith of the Church, the Church comes to faith by being inserted into the faith of Christ himself. For the fact of the matter is that we stand before God, as we were called by God, in, with and through Christ.

Jesus, insofar as he shared our human condition, shared our vocation to hear the call of God and to respond to it in obedient living and dying. Like us, he had to live an open-ended faith, being led, day-by-day, by the will of the God he called confidently, "Abba." If this were not clear enough from the Gospels, it is made quite explicit by the Letter to the Hebrews:

> In the days of his flesh, Jesus offered up prayers and supplications, with loud cries and tears, to him who alone was able to save him from death, and he was heard for his godly fear. Although he was Son, he learned obedience through suffering; and, being made perfect, he became the source of eternal salvation to all who obey him (5:7–12).

Or again:

> . . . let us run with perseverance the race that is set before us, looking to Jesus, the pioneer and perfecter of our faith, who, for the joy that was set before him, endured the cross, despising the shame, and is seated at the right hand of God (12:1–2).

Thus, what we call the paschal mystery can also be understood, in terms of Jesus' inner life, as his life of faith whereby, in all the events and circumstances of his life—even to death on a cross—he totally and freely entrusted himself into the hands of God who alone could deliver him out of death. His whole life was such a life: and all his relationships—to the Romans and the

Sanhedrin, to his family and his disciples, to the crowds and to his enemies—were marked by this faithful obedience.

That, too, is the faith of the Church, its conformity to Christ. *That*, and no other, is the faith of the Church, celebrated in its liturgy, lived in its life, manifest in its works, articulated (though never exhaustively or finally) in its teachings and discipline, and drawing it into God's future. It is into this faith of Christ as lived by the Church that the catechumen is initiated and eventually baptized.

By way of conclusion, two further remarks are in order.

First, since faith in God is precisely not faith in ourselves or our own abilities, it is inherent in true faith that it should acknowledge that God is doing something for us and in us which we cannot do for ourselves. To come to true faith is to experience the saving presence of God in our lives as pure gift and to be shaken free from our attachment to gods who cannot save in order to serve the living God. Faith is our response to God's saving self-disclosure to us, but the response itself is as much gift of God as it is our own free commitment. Hence the importance of the stories of the catechumens and the stories of the Church, both of which depict the partnership of faith, a mystery defying easy analysis in terms of allocating the respective roles of grace and human freedom, yet one whose real and liberating character is patent in the stories of faith. Moreover, since the catechumens' stories of faith are also stories of God's gracious presence and power, they represent at least one dimension of God's continuing presence to his Church. Consequently, it is not just a matter of the catechumens learning of God from the Church; the Church must also learn of God from discerning his revealing activity in the lives of the catechumens.

Second, it is worth reminding ourselves of the "sacramental" quality of both revelation and faith. In the present, as in the past, God's self-revelation and our faith response are essentially, even primarily, embodied in actions and events,whose meaning is apprehended in reflection and articulated in words. They are, as the catechism says, "visible signs of invisible graces"; or, in the words of the *Decree on Divine Revelation*, word and event are so related that "the deeds wrought by God in the history of revelation manifest and confirm the teachings and realities pro-claimed by the words, while the words proclaim the deeds and clarify the mystery contained in them" (n. 2). The saving word and our faithful response have always to be "made flesh," to take on particular concrete form in the lives of real people. This pri-ority of God in faith and its necessarily "enacted" form are what serve to link faith and sacraments together in such a way that each necessarily requires the other.

3. *Faith and Belief*

Before going on to explore the role of sacraments and rites in the process of faith, it might be well to consider the relation of the life of faith to the matter of belief.

Since the Creed is usually taken as a summary of Christian beliefs and used as such to structure catechumenal programs, it is instructive to note that the original home of the Creed is in the liturgy, as part of an *action*. Although its place in the present baptismal liturgy precedes the actual baptismal action, the threefold interrogation of faith originally took place in the font itself. In the earliest Roman tradition (*The Apostolic Tradition of Hippolytus*, c. 215), the candidate stands in the water and is asked three times "Do you believe . . . ?" Each time, after saying "I believe" (*credo*), the candidate is plunged into the water. This is not just a last minute effort to be sure the candidate has un-derstood the religious instructions. The words proclaim the meaning of the action, while the action confirms and manifests the meaning of the words. The candidate identifies with Christ in submitting to God in faith, even unto death: "Do you not know that all of us who have been baptized into Christ Jesus have been baptized into his death?" (Rom 6:3) The obedience sacramentalized in Christ's death on the cross is the same obedi-ence of faith to which the neophyte surrenders, an obedience irrevocably pledged to God's word for the sake of the joy that lies ahead. It is an act of God who does what we cannot do for ourselves: he delivers us from ourselves and from the death that we might live in freedom.

Unfortunately, the detachment of the Creed from the bap-tismal liturgy has given it a life of its own and led it to be seen primarily as a convenient summary of all the things the Christian is to believe. In a lengthy study, entitled *Faith and Belief,* Wilfred Cantwell Smith has traced this evolution. He points out that the history of the term *credo* indicates that its original Christian meaning was "to designate an act of self-commitment in which the will was predominant," and that only later did it come to be associated primarily with the mind. "This word, it seems, is a compound from *cor, cordis,* 'heart' (as in English, 'cordial,' 'accord,' 'concord' and the like . . .) plus *do,* 'put, place, set,' and also 'give.' . . . There would be little question but that as a crucial term in a crucial liturgical act of personal engagement—namely Christian baptism—*credo* came close to its root meaning of 'I set my heart on,' 'I give my heart to' . . . or, more generally: 'I hereby commit myself' . . . 'I pledge allegiance.' "[5] Interestingly enough, something of the same idea underlies the etymology of the English term "belief" which, as Cantwell Smith points out, is related to the old English word "lief," expressing preference, and to the German *belieben,* meaning to consider lovely, to like, to wish for, to choose.

These reflections on the origins of "creed" and "belief" show that their earliest meanings were identical with what we have argued to be the meaning of "faith": an option of loving submission to the God who reveals and saves. But what connection has this to the "truths of faith"?

Perhaps it would be better to speak of the "mysteries" of faith, for the term "mystery" better expresses what we mean when we say we believe in the incarnation, or the Trinity, or the immaculate conception. Here the term "mystery" means more than an intellectual puzzle: it means the plan of God unfolding in human history, which plan is discerned in specific events upon which the Christian life rests. To recognize the birth of Jesus as the mystery of the incarnation, for example, is to find in the stories of this event, and in the person whose birth is not only remembered but celebrated, a saving self-disclosure of God by which our own life of faith is to be oriented. We do not so much believe in concepts, such as "incarnation" or "immaculate conception," but we trust the stories which these terms sum up. In them, we find our own experience of the

world and of God prefigured and identified. To trust in these
stories is to live by them. In this way, the story of our own lives
becomes part of the larger story of what God has done, is doing
and will yet do, because God is faithful. Thus, the "mysteries of
faith" are to be approached neither as mere "facts about the
world" nor as religious brain-teasers, but as stories to be entered
into as revealing how God is calling us to stand before him and
how we are to respond. It is for this reason, surely, that the
RCIA requires that the formation of the catechumens be accommodated to the liturgical year (i.e., march in step with the community of the faithful as they live out these stories together) and
lead the catechumens "to a suitable knowledge of dogmas and
precepts and also to *an intimate understanding of the mystery of salvation in which they desire to share*" (n. 19, 1; emphasis added). An
intimate understanding, like an intimate conversation or an intimate friendship, is "heart to heart."

Finally, in reflecting upon the liturgical-baptismal context
of the profession of faith, Cantwell Smith makes two concluding
points which refer equally to the process of coming to faith and
to its ritualization in baptism.

> The first, obvious enough, is the self-transformational
> character of the action. The initiate was taking on a
> new life, with baptism as the implicating sign of his or
> her becoming involved in it. Thus one was taking an
> existentially decisive step: one of utter self-commit-
> ment. In this act one was engaging oneself. The words
> were performative.
>
> Secondly, we may note a certain polarity in the
> matter, giving rise to a double possibility of view-point.
> Through baptism . . . the person was leaving a world of
> atomistic disorder for a new and divine world of liber-
> ating service to God: one was oneself choosing the lat-
> ter and one was being welcomed into it. From one
> point of view, accordingly, the emphasis was on this
> decision, on one's dedication of one's own person to the
> new venture. From the other side, the magnificent
> availability of the new order could be stressed, the

readiness of God to receive one. The momentous decision—it was starkly that—could be sensed as something that in the one case one strikingly made, and that
in the other was astonishingly enabled to make.[6]

Thus coming to faith is both our struggle and, simultaneously, God's power at work in us. Hence the traditional
teaching that faith is a supernatural gift, itself an act of God and
not merely a human response to God disclosing himself. We
must not think of ourselves as over against God, as equal partners, but of ourselves awakening to the beckoning presence of
God in whom we have always lived, moved and had our being.
This delicate engagement of grace and freedom, of divine initiative and human response, is difficult to resolve theoretically, as
the history of the controversies over grace reveal; but it is important to respect its occurrence in life and to avoid organizing
the catechumenate in such a way as to give the impression that
all that matters is for the converts to swear acceptance to a set of
propositions. The Church's teaching on faith and morals are attempts, sometimes but not always inspired, to indicate the art of
living the life of faith.

4. *Faith and the Catechumenate.*
Perhaps we can summarize our findings so far in a series of
conclusions which might serve to guide the conducting of a catechumenate:

1. *Faith is universal and therefore ambivalent.* A central concern of the catechumenate will be to allow the Gospel to cast its
light into the depths of our hearts so that false faiths can be recognized and rejected in favor of faith in the God who revealed
himself in Christ and who continues to offer his saving self-disclosure to men and women of today.

2. *Faith is theological.* Faith is one of the three theological virtues, for its object is God alone: the God who creates and sus-
tains our world, who is present to it still, who calls us to trust
not in ourselves or in any creature, but in him alone, and who

continues to raise up those who are bowed down in the image of his Son whom he delivered out of death.

3. *Faith is eschatological.* Faith is a fundamental orientation of one's life, a life which has to be lived out into an unknown future. The faithful person is always in process, moving toward that final and total transformation to which we are called and which we identify as "the resurrection of the dead and the life of the world to come." So faith is not so much something we hold as something which holds us and transforms us more and more into the likeness of Christ, throughout life's gracious and dangerous vicissitudes.

4. *Faith is sacramental.* It resides not in the mind alone, but in the whole person. It therefore transcends our ability to grasp it or articulate it fully, but it is revealed in our total life-style and life-story. It is in our continual interaction with ourself, with other selves and with the material universe that we discover who we are and the faith we live by; and conversely, in the same process we exercise our freedom to shape our lives and our world by living in trusting obedience toward God and embodying that in the choices we make.

5. *Faith is gift.* Our relationship with God is entirely dependent upon his gracious initiative toward us, as a result of which we discover him doing in us what we could not do for ourselves.

6. *The catechumen already belongs to the household of faith.* If the catechumen already belongs to the Church (RCIA #18) this is not to be understood merely in a juridical sense, but as an acknowledgement that he or she already lives by the faith of Christ. This has the effect of giving the catechumen certain claims upon the community of faith, but it also modifies our conception of what constitutes membership in the Church. Thus the Church must always expect to be confronted with the challenge faced by Peter in the person of Cornelius and his household, namely, the challenge to acknowledge the spirit at work in arousing true faith even outside the juridical boundaries of the visible Church.

II. Sacraments

As we noted earlier, there seems to be some uncertainty abroad as to the role of the ritual elements in the catechumenate. To put the problem bluntly: if the catechumens are already living by faith, experiencing the saving power of God in their lives and confessing their faith in word and action, what do the sacraments add? The temptation is to revert to a quasi-magical account of the sacraments in explaining why they are necessary, or else to reduce the sacramental celebrations to celebrations of the faith-journey where, like secular celebrations, they are tacked on to something—like a promotion—that has already happened independently of them. The challenge is to try to transcend this dichotomy, both parts of which reveal a real impoverishment of sacramental understanding.

1. *The Sacraments of Faith*

It should be remarked from the outset that the term "sacrament" will be used here in a sense wider than that of the "matter" and "form," wider than that of the seven sacraments, to include all the liturgical celebrations of the catechumenate. These celebrations include what might be called the "transition rites" (becoming catechumen, election, the Easter sacraments) and the "intensification rites" (exorcisms, blessings, scrutinies, giving of the Creed and the Lord's Prayer, the celebrations of the word in the catechumenate and the Easter celebrations of Eucharist in the period of mystagogy). This is not to put them all on an equal footing—any more than all the seven sacraments are themselves on an equal footing—but it is to suggest that they are all to be seen as ecclesial acts of worship and sanctification, effected through the presence of the Spirit of Christ. It is also to suggest that they are to be seen as source and summit, or at least mini-sources and mini-summits, of the broader sacramentality of the process of divine encounter and human response which we have noted in the journey of faith itself.

On the other hand, it is precisely the "sacramental" quality of faith itself, and the corresponding claim that the catechumen already lives by faith and is sanctified by God in Christ through the Spirit, which raises the question: What do the sacramental celebrations of the Church *add*? To this two things may be said by way of beginning to elaborate an answer.

First, the rites of the Church heighten our awareness of what is at stake in the life of faith upon which we are embarked. God's gracious intervention in human life is not restricted to explicitly liturgical moments. The whole experience of the catechumenate enables us to recognize that God may break into our lives on occasions as mundane as a chance encounter with a stranger or a catechumenal session with coffee and doughnuts. In the saying and doing of human interaction, God may be found to have spoken and acted. While the liturgy shares the same structure of saying and doing and makes the same claim to mediate an encounter with God, the *ritualized* character of the event means that we are set up for this encounter. This being "set up" for encounter with God is the effect of the objectivity of the ritual and especially of its doxological character. The objectivity of the ritual requires us to enter into it, as if entering into a larger space than that of our own personal existence. The doxological character of the rite means that it puts certain words of confession and acknowledgement on our lips which not only express what we know and feel, but even more importantly draw us into a more profound knowing and feeling. The words and gestures of the rite bring us to stand at the end of human action and language, till we tremble on the edge of that ultimately unnameable and unmanageable mystery we call God. That real presence of the mystery of God confronted in the liturgy is what we call its *ex opere operato* character; the readiness to attend to that mystery and to submit to it is the *opus operantis*, the subjective character of the rite. Of course, the same real, saving presence of God is to be found in all of life, and continually demands of us the appropriate *opus operantis* of awareness and response, but in the liturgy the ritual directs our awareness and leads us to a fuller, more appropriate response.

A second dimension of the liturgical rites which needs to be recognized is their *performative* character. The concept of performativity was developed in language studies to account for the fact that when we speak we not only describe a state of affairs which exists or might exist, but we actually *do* something, as often as not; i.e. we bring a state of affairs into existence. Thus, under appropriate circumstances, words *work:* as when a bride and groom say "I do," or a jury is sworn in, or a contract is ratified, or a ship is launched, or two people make a bet. In these instances, the saying does not describe how people feel inwardly: it has the effect of altering their relationship with one another and with society. They can, for example, be held accountable and punished for false speaking, for such ritual speaking constitutes the very network of social existence and perjury or disregard of the conventions would only serve to destroy the social fabric.

So with the liturgy of the Church: its words and gestures, too, are performative and thus really efficacious, for they have the effect of reordering our relationships in such a way as to make them the kind of relationships that belong to the Kingdom and thus signs of God's victorious presence in human life. Words of exorcism and renunciation both represent and effect a break with an old network of relationships (the "world"); blessings, presentations of the Creed and the Lord's Prayer, the Ephphatha rite, the anointings, the celebration of baptism, confirmation and Eucharist, represent and effect our appropriation of our new role.

The importance of the concept of performativity in speech and gesture lies in its insight that we are social beings whose identity is established by our relationships and not merely by some independent, interior sense of who we are; and that, furthermore, language and gesture have the ability not merely to describe relationships already established, but to create and modify relationships. Thus our interior life is shaped and conditioned by the network of real and objective relations which make up each person's world, and the relations are created, enacted and transformed by the rituals of speech and gesture which mediate social life. So, for example, rituals of greeting create bonds, while rituals of insult destroy them. To participate in a Fourth of July parade is to affirm one's identification with the "world" represented by that day and its pageants. To marry is publicly, symbolically and very really to break with one set of relationships in order to enter into another. It is "only" a matter of words and gestures, but the effects are real. We are changed in the alteration of our relationships; we are constituted, affirmed and transformed in and through our rituals, which affect us profoundly as persons whose identity is established in relationship.

Thus the ritual of the RCIA is celebrated for the purposes of altering our identity, it might be said. But the new identity is no easier to grasp than the old: we assume it, but we do not know it exhaustively. The reason for this is obvious: not only does God remain a mystery, but we even remain something of a mystery to ourselves. Thus the meaning of the new identity is to be discovered in living it out. All that happens in the liturgy is that there is an encounter which, if we engage in it with anything more than merely superficial attention, must make us aware of the mystery and of the real change of identity which results from the rite. This acknowledgement of the mystery of God and this acceptance of our new identity corresponds to the double movement of the sacrament, a double movement which is usually described as sanctification and as worship.

2. *Sacraments as Worship and Sanctification*

To speak of the sacramental liturgy as being constituted both by worship and by sanctification is to speak of our relationship to God, mediated by Christ in the Church, as reciprocal. Worship of God here implies public acknowledgement of the God of one's life: "I will tell of thy name to my brethren; in the midst of the congregation I will praise thee" (Ps 22:22). Sanctification in liturgy means that people are transformed, in that their relationship to the world, to their fellow-believers and to God is altered: they become new and different people with a new identity to be lived out. But it is important to remember what has been said already about the way both God and our own real selves transcend the ideas we have of God or the image we have of ourselves. Thus to praise God is always to say more than we know; to be a Christian is to receive an identity whose full implications remain to be explored. Like faith itself, liturgy is open-ended, and for the same reasons. Like our faith, our worship is the worship of the Church and ultimately the worship of Christ; and the new identity we receive in the rites is ultimately none other than the identity of Christ, through his body the Church.

Just as the Church has always insisted that faith is a grace, the gift of God rather than any human achievement, so it has always insisted likewise upon the "objective" character of the grace of the sacraments. It should be possible now to see more clearly what is meant by that and perhaps even to appreciate what is meant by the claim that the gift of faith is given in the sacrament itself.

The same person who submits to becoming part of the faith of the Church, knowing the life of faith to be something to be grown into, will also know that liturgical prayer is not the simultaneous prayer of several hundred individuals all giving thanks for their own private blessings, but the prayer of the one people, transcending yet including each and every individual. We lend our hearts and bodies to the Church, so that it can praise God for the loving kindness shown to all humanity. Similarly, the sanctification of the faithful is never the sanctification of one individual. Even if it should be only one infant being baptized at the Easter vigil, the sanctificaton of that child is inseparable from the sanctification of all present: for sanctification, as we saw, is always and necessarily transformation of identity through change of relationships. It takes only one person to be baptized and all relationships are (in principle) altered. Thus, in the RCIA, the public celebration of all the rituals is not merely for the sake of the converts, but also for the sake of the assembled faithful; we, too, are changed by this new sacramental event. Sacramental acts, as acts of worship and sanctification, are both acts *of* and acts *for* the Church as a whole.

But, as we also saw earlier, the Church's relationship to God is not immediate; it is always in, with and through Christ. So the worship of the Church, its acknowledgement of God, is not independent of Jesus' own worship of the Father. Rather, the individual enters into the worship of the Church, knowing it to be the right way to stand before God; but the Church stands rightly before God by offering, not its own worship, but the prayer and worship of Christ himself. Similarly, though this may sound more strange, as the individual is not sanctified except in the Church being sanctified, so the Church is only sanctified insofar as God sanctifies Jesus. Insofar as the power of God to transform the human condition was visible in the life and death of Jesus, and above all in raising Jesus from the dead, so that same power which was at work in Christ is now at work in the Church and in the individual believer. We are being transformed into the Church which is being transformed into Christ who is our peace and reconciliation with God. The Spirit who raised Christ Jesus from the dead and established him in glory will raise our mortal bodies also; but in the meantime, during the Church's pilgrimage of faith, we are being transformed into the likeness of Christ, from glory to glory, through the Spirit which is in him (cf. 2 Cor 3:18).

Thus Christ is the key to a proper understanding of both faith and sacraments. Neither can be divorced from the Spirit of Christ who draws the Church into the faith and liturgy of Christ himself: it is in the Church's faith and liturgy that we come to Christ; it is in Christ's faith and liturgy that we come to God in worship and God comes to us in sanctification.

3. *The Rites of Christian Initiation*

If the approach to faith and sacrament outlined here has any validity, it must affect the way the RCIA is implemented. It might be useful to conclude by offering some considerations which could assist those charged with the implementation of the RCIA.

1. *Ritual is ambivalent.* We saw that not all faith is Christian faith and that even religious faith can be distorted. The same is true of Christian ritual. Christian ritual can be used (unconsciously) by individuals to protect themselves from the risks and insecurity of genuine faith, as when they are understood to operate in some magical fashion which makes personal commitment or conversion of life unnecessary. Ritual can be distorted (unconsciously) by Christian communities whose theory or practice of the sacraments either encourages a magical under-

standing of the rites or reduces them to a means of teaching or to a means of community affirmation.

2. *Ritual is open-ended.* In contrast to our propensity to explain the meaning of the sacraments beforehand, it is remarkable that teaching on the sacraments of initiation was frequently reserved in the early Church until *after* the catechumens had been sacramentally initiated. As Cyril of Jerusalem told his neophytes: "I long ago wanted to tell you about these spiritual and heavenly mysteries ... but, knowing well that seeing is more persuasive than hearing, I have waited until now."[7] This is not to propose that we slavishly return to the practice of an earlier age, but merely that we remember that the understanding of baptism, for example, derives from being baptized and not from having it all spelled out beforehand. It is a personal encounter and, like all personal encounters, no amount of preparation can really prepare a person for what to expect. Consequently, sacramental catechesis must be conducted primarily by the neophytes themselves reflecting upon their experience under the guidance of the Church and its Scriptures. Any previous instruction must be careful not to presume to be able to say ahead of time what the sacraments will mean, but rather attempt to prepare the candidates to be as attentive and receptive to the words and symbols as possible.

3. *Ritual is there to be observed.* Our experience of liturgical change these last twenty years, plus the multiplicity of options given in the reformed rites, may have given the impression that liturgy is something we can create for ourselves. But ritual, like language, is less something we create for ourselves than something we inherit. We do not make it up as we go along, but we learn to live in it creatively by submitting to its structures and symbols. It is true for us, as it is true for the catechumens, that we learn the meaning of the rites by carrying them out, as we learn the riches of the English language by using it as respectfully as we know how. Thus, if we are not sure what to make of the rite of dismissing the catechumens at the end of the liturgy of the word, for example, perhaps we should try it with a view

to discovering why it should have been suggested to us. Similarly, we should be slow to drop or alter parts of the ritual on the grounds that it doesn't mean anything: the fault may just lie in ourselves.

4. *Catechumens need to be introduced to the art of liturgical prayer.* Despite the lip-service paid to the centrality of the liturgy in the life of the Church and the life of the Christian, it is striking how almost everything said or written about prayer today still focuses more or less exclusively upon private and personal prayer. The insistence of the RCIA that the formation of catechumens be accommodated to the liturgical year and enriched by celebrations of the word, and that they be helped on their journey of faith by suitable liturgical rites (RCIA #19), points to the importance of their being initiated to the art of praying in and with the Church. While there is no space here for elaborating what that might mean, it is to be hoped that these reflections on the nature of Christian faith and the character of Christian ritual will go some way at least to providing a basis for the practice of liturgical prayer.

Notes

1. Tertullian, *On Baptism*, 2.
2. James Fowler, "Perspectives on the Family from the Standpoint of Faith Development Theory," *Perkins Journal*, Fall 1979, p. 7.
3. Juan Mateos, S.J., "The Message of Jesus," *Sojourners*, July 1977, pp. 8–16.
4. Robin Scroggs, *Paul for a New Day*. Philadelphia: Fortress Press, 1977, p. 26.
5. Wilfred Cantwell Smith, *Faith and Belief*. Princeton, N.J.: Princeton University Press, 1979, p. 76.
6. *Ibid.*, pp. 74–75.
7. Cyril of Jerusalem, *Mystagogical Catechesis* I, 1.

The Rites and Rituals of Commitment

Regis A. Duffy, O.F.M.

St. Paul, like many other Christians of his day, took sacraments seriously. Although the Christians of the first century had not been brought through a lengthy catechumenate such as may have existed at Rome or Carthage a hundred years later, the house-churches and communities of Christians certainly seemed to have called out fervent conviction and commitment from their converts. Paul's constant refrain about how Christians are experiencing salvation because the message of the cross has been accepted (1 Cor 1:18) is a commentary on their commitment. Like Paul, we will assume a necessary connection between Gospel conversion and commitment throughout this article.

An interesting historical and sociological question would be how these communities were able to evoke such commitment in a short period of time and in difficult situations. But our concern is a contemporary pastoral one: How is the catechumenate a practical model for calling out commitment for the ecclesial and sacramental life of Christians today? Initiation which the catechumenate prepares candidates for is the model for all other worship and sacrament.

Are the sacraments of initiation, however, being confused with other rites of passage in our society?[1] Car keys and the right to order a drink are identified as rites of passage by some American teenagers. Graduation from college and buying one's first car are viewed as similar transitional rites by segments of America's young adults. Built into these and other public rites of passage are the assumptions and expectations of both the young and their elders.

When rites which invite and celebrate participants' passage from one stage of life or position in the community to another are performed in a compact and highly structured group, the meaning and transformations of that society can still attain their purpose. Rites of passage for a teenager, for example, even in increasingly Westernized sections of Africa, may still have a powerful impact that renews the group in initiating the candidate.

But in our American culture, traditional religious rites of passage (e.g., First Communion, confirmation, marriage) tend to get confused or blurred with other public rituals of American life (e.g., graduation and anniversaries), nor are they necessarily celebrated in tightly knit family or ecclesial structures. In fact, pastoral praxis may unwittingly encourage this same unfocused and uncommitted ritualization in the way sacraments are celebrated. Infant baptism or marriage, for example, which require little or no re-examination or commitment to the Gospel way of life perpetuate this problem of rites with largely secular meanings celebrated as Christian sacraments.

This article will deal with two related issues: the quality of commitment required and evoked by sacrament and how this commitment is expressed in the symbols, rituals, and commitments of the RCIA. The emphasis throughout this discussion will be on the praxis (i.e., the doing) of sacrament in the process of conversion called the RCIA. Our theological theories often enough are not reflected in the ways we celebrate commitment and conversion. It is important, then, that we analyze the pastoral contexts in which conversion is actually lived out and that we know when our theories and praxis have little to do with one another.

Contexts of Sacrament

The Church did not begin its ministry in the first century with theoretical definitions of sacrament. Rather, Christian communities were shaped by the shared meanings and purposes that the cross and resurrection of Jesus summed up. When Paul remembers how he began the Christian community at Corinth, for example, he outlines this process: ". . . when I came to you I did not come proclaiming God's testimony with any particular eloquence or 'wisdom.' No, I determined that while I was with you I would speak of nothing but Jesus Christ and him crucified. . . . As a consequence, your faith rests not on the wisdom of men but on the power of God" (1 Cor 2:1–2, 5).

Since many of us have come from institutionalized experiences of Christianity, we can easily forget how different the process of sharing, proclaiming, and celebrating the meaning of Christ's self-gift for all people is from circulating and repeating definitions and theories about the cross of Christ. This process of sharing meaning helped these first Christians clarify what God was doing in their midst and transformed a motley group of individuals into a credible community: "Consider your situation. Not many of you are wise, as men account wisdom; not many are influential; and surely not many are well-born. . . . God it is who has given you life in Christ Jesus. He has made him our wisdom and also our justice, our sanctification, and our redemption" (1 Cor 1:26, 30).

In other words, the central teaching of the cross of Christ was experienced as a process in which people were challenged and enabled to revise radically their basic attitudes, values, and relationships. Their self-awareness as a Church, the "body of Christ," was rooted in this same process. In practical terms the meaning of the cross entailed a challenge to "acquire a fresh, spiritual way of thinking" (Eph 4:23).

In Paul's thinking, the cross radically transforms the ways we are together now and in God's Kingdom. This Pauline teaching is called justification: "Just as through one man's disobedience all became sinners, so through one man's obedience all shall become just" (Rom 5:19). Paul is not proposing a theory about how God saves us. Rather, he is witnessing to what he sees happening in the imperfect Christian communities that he has founded, ministered in, or heard about. In Chapter 6 of Romans, Paul sketches the results of God's unearned and justifying love: everything is possible because God is part of our lives.

But the cross does not effect a series of privately saved individuals. Through Christ's self-gift a saving community is finally possible. Sin reinforces the alienation and division that make community impossible. Reconciliation through the cross of Christ brings people together in saving ways for the sake of others: "This means that you are strangers and aliens no longer. No, you are fellow citizens of the saints and members of the household of God. You form a building which rises on the foundation of the apostles and prophets, with Christ Jesus himself as the capstone. Through him the whole structure is fitted together and takes shape as a holy temple in the Lord; in him you are being built into this temple to become a dwelling place for God in the Spirit" (Eph 2:19–22).

There are many ways of analyzing the climate of such communities, but Victor Turner's use of Arnold van Gennep's classic description of "rites of passage" is probably the most useful for our purposes. Turner suggests that the ideal way to be together is "communitas." This type of community, as opposed to other social groupings, is characterized by a more spontaneous and open way of being together as they interact and tear down the structures that keep them apart.[2] Such communities are never permanently achieved but rather require the constant effort of renewal and rites of passage.

Turner, however, has pinpointed a crucial dynamic of renewal in such communities, that of "liminality," in which there is a temporary separation from the security of our previous roles and tasks in preparation for assuming a new place in the community. I have described this process elsewhere as "musical chairs" because ultimately not only the neophytes and candidates but the initiated as well must once more reassess their current position and move into other stages and challenges.[3] Put another way, communities that fulfill their promise of helping people be together in better ways continue to call out the needed gifts and roles of their members.

Initiation: Rite of Passage

The sacraments of initiation in the early Christian communities can be described as rites of passage which symbolized the death and resurrection of Jesus and the Christian's entry into the same experience. At the same time, the power of Christ's death was not separated from the gift of the Spirit. It was this Spirit which brought Christians together: "It was *in one Spirit* that all of us, whether Jew or Greek, slave or free, were *baptized into one body*" (1 Cor 12:13). This "body" was not simply a social metaphor but, often enough, "a concrete allusion to the human body of Jesus, crucified and raised from the dead."[4]

In brief, early Christian communities were continually formed and reformed by a dynamic understanding of how the death and resurrection of Jesus brought them together in the Spirit as "Church" or body of Christ. The rites which celebrated these beliefs might resemble initiation rites of other contemporary pagan societies in some ways, but the cross of Christ marked these Christian communities in a unique fashion.[5] The cross was the dividing point between the Christian community and superficially similar associations. The cross for these first churches was the ultimate symbol of commitment.

The cross motivated the morality of the community: "His death was death to sin, once for all; his life is life for God. In the same way, you must consider yourself dead to sin but alive to God in Christ Jesus. Do not, therefore, let sin rule your mortal body and make you obey its lusts. . . . Rather, offer yourselves to God as men who have come back from the dead to life, and your bodies to God as weapons for justice" (Rom 6:10–13).

The profile of such early Christian communities begins to emerge more sharply. In the Pauline communities, for example, commitment to the Gospel way of life and its mission to others is to be rooted in the initiation experience of dying and rising with Christ. Candidates in the Christian house-church of Stephanas (1 Cor 16:15ff), of Chloe (1 Cor 1:11), or Aristobulus and Narcissus (Rom 16:10ff) would find imperfect but committed Christians who had, in various degrees, appropriated the message of the cross of Christ in practical ways of living, sharing, and praying. Their familial language to one another ("brother/ sister") marked this shared commitment.

Within such communities, worship and the sacraments were an experience, not a theory. The Corinthians, for example, seem to have misunderstood the meaning of what they celebrated in initiation and Eucharist. What they were doing (praxis) in sacrament inevitably overflowed into other areas of their shared life: "First of all, I hear that when you gather for a meeting there are divisions among you, and I am inclined to believe it. . . . When you assemble it is not to eat the Lord's Supper, for everyone is in haste to eat his own supper. One person goes hungry while another gets drunk" (1 Cor 11:18, 20–21).

The situation at Corinth was all the more serious precisely because these Christians were drawing the wrong meaning from the sacraments they were celebrating. The cross of Christ seems to have been regarded as a safely remote historical event which was ritualized in initiation and Eucharist but had no impact on their current lives. Paul's sharp reminder is an attempt to correct this self-serving interpretation: "Every time, then, you eat this bread and drink this cup, you proclaim the death of the Lord until he comes" (1 Cor 11:26). A major test of whether this teaching is being lived is the unity of the community: "Because the loaf of bread is one, we, many though we are, are one body for we all partake of the one loaf" (1 Cor 10:17). The cross is the source of Christian community and mission because it calls out shared commitment to be like Christ.

Let me suggest some practical corollaries of our discussion so far. First, everything that we do (praxis) and believe must result in the renewal of the Christian community that Paul calls the "body of Christ." When this task is lost sight of, the results are a weakening of the sense of Gospel mission in the community and privatized sacraments. Second, the cross and resurrection of Jesus are, first and foremost, the radical and continuing experience (not theory) of the Christian community and its members. This experience must shape the community's awareness of why they receive sacraments. Third, what the Christian community celebrates and does may not necessarily be the same as the theory or doctrine it officially teaches. Candidates may be told, for example, that they are baptized into the death of Christ (theory), but the attitudes of the community and its individuals may not reflect this teaching in actual practice. When there is a wide and consistent gap between theory and praxis in the Christian community, the credibility of the mission of that group is threatened.

Meanings of Sacrament

Sacraments are never isolated from the Christian communities which celebrate them. Just as the Church, as body of Christ, is called to continue the reconciling work of Christ (2 Cor 5:14–21), so the sacraments are the symbols of his presence empowering that mission and ministry. At the heart of Paul's teaching on sacrament, then, is the conviction that in initiation we follow the same road as Christ: "Through baptism into his death we were buried with him, so that, just as Christ was raised from the dead by the glory of the Father, we too might live a new life. If we have been united with him through likeness to his death, so shall we be through a like resurrection" (Rom 6:4–5). Because of this shared experience with Christ, Christians are united in their shared commitment to God's purpose and vision for his renewed creation. Sacraments enable us to participate in God's work of shaping his "new creation."

In the root experience of sacrament, initiation, Christians are enabled to be like Christ so as to do as Christ: to proclaim the good news of God's salvation. But the Church of each historical period has the responsibility of discerning what this shared mission of Christians entails in its own time and cultural situation. We see Paul, for example, helping the church at Corinth to discern the practical implications of its Christian commitment in his letters to them. In a similar way, the national conference of American bishops may give general guidelines on questions of evangelization or nuclear disarmament, but the local church must once again translate its baptismal commitment into practical assessment and applications of these guidelines to Gospel living. All sacramental life in a Christian community empowers its members to share in this Gospel.

A sacrament includes, then, not only what God does but, as a result, what we are empowered to do in his name. In the theory of sacraments, this twofold aspect of sacrament was eventually described as the objective (*ex opere operato*) and subjective (*ex opere operantis*) dimensions of sacrament. God's unearned and reconciling gift of salvation is the continuing basis of every sacrament celebrated within the Church.[6] Neither the minister's nor the recipient's worthiness merits such a gift.

On the other hand, God's gifts are given to effect his purposes. An honest and committed reception of any sacrament includes the willingness to share in Christ's work. But we always accept the strength of Christ to serve the Gospel from the imperfect situation of our current stage of life. Expressed another way, Christ's presence in sacrament enables us to respond in sacrament. The result of such a dialogue is renewed commitment in which we hear Paul's words now addressed to us: "As your fellow workers we beg you not to receive the grace of God in vain" (2 Cor 6:1).

The history of the term "sacrament" is a complex one. Tertullian, for example, the third century North African theologian who did so much to develop this term, sometimes uses "sacrament" to translate the New Testament expression for the mystery of God's presence. He also employs the term in the sense understood by his contemporaries—the soldier's oath of allegiance to the emperor: "We are now called to the military service of the living God when we respond in the words of sacrament" (*To the Martyrs*, 3).

The underlying idea is that of a commitment made to Christ. Tertullian reiterates this same notion of commitment even more clearly in a famous passage: "We are not baptized so that we may cease committing sin but because we have ceased, since we are already clean of heart. This, surely, is the first baptism of the catechumen."[7]

Sacrament, then, calls out commitment to God's view of things as revealed in the cross and resurrection of Christ. This Christian commitment is renewed and deepened as the community tries to be faithful to its tasks in settings as different as the slums of a large American city or a college campus, and as individual Christians reassess their priorities and values in the transitional crises of each stage of life.

At this point, if we reconsider the rites of passage discussed earlier, it is easier, perhaps, to see their connection with sacrament. Within the Church community, sacraments are rites of passage which both challenge and help Christians to reappropriate the meaning and mission of salvation for themselves and their world. The Christian rites of passage for teenagers, for example, have a different and, hopefully, larger purpose than those of their cultural group. For a young American adult to appropriate freely the cross of Christ and its meaning, peer group and even elders' values may have to be re-examined and, perhaps, discarded. It is hard to believe that the example of a young naked Francis of Assisi, casting aside his father's bourgeois values, is the exception in the history of Christian commitment.

What happens, however, to the process of building up the body of Christ in the local church when operational definitions of sacrament have little or nothing to do with conversion and mission? If confirmation and marriage, for example, have become routine rites of ethnic belonging to a group called "the Church" which require no deepening commitment to the Gospel, how does this tear down the body of Christ?

Intending Sacraments

For nearly two thousand years, the continuing pastoral question about the sacramental life of the Church has been: Do we mean what Christ means in receiving a sacrament? As already suggested, this question is answered in the way the Christian community and individual Christians within it live and proclaim the Gospel message.

Just as Paul can urge the Corinthian Christians, for example, that "whether you eat or drink—whatever you do—you should do all for the glory of God" (1 Cor 10:31), so the reverse is also possible: attitudes, accompanying our worship and sacraments, which do not give glory to God. Paul cites a crucial example: "What I now have to say is not said in praise, because your meetings are not profitable but harmful" (1 Cor 11:17). Ritually, initiation and Eucharist at Corinth were no doubt similar in their celebration to that of other Christian communities. Paul detects, however, an incomplete understanding of these sacraments, judging by the results of the Corinthian praxis.

Intention has to do with the way in which we "own" our commitments.[8] By their very nature, commitments must be renewed and deepened if they are to focus effectively our efforts and resources. Just as the public rituals of July 4 and Thanksgiving and the family rituals of birthdays and anniversaries should celebrate a continuing dedication and commitment to certain values and meanings in our lives, so the sacramental celebrations of what Christ does among us must bring us back to the familiar landscape of our lives with new vision and firmer purpose.

But it is easy for the Church and the individual Christian to forget that intentions can only be made within the context of our current life-stage and our past experience. In other words, we cannot be committed apart from the narratives of our experience and God's influence there. The very commitments that the forty year old Christian is called to make may be blocked or aided by the way in which other key commitments were worked through as a young adult. For this same Christian to "intend" the sacrament of marriage requires much deeper commitment and resources than when first married fifteen years previously.

In both the teaching and the ministry of sacraments there is always the temptation to emphasize the objective meaning of Christ's presence without ever attending to the question of our presence or the lack of it in these familiar rituals. The result can be a good deal of moralizing about the meaning of sacraments in abstract and generalized categories which do not clarify the actual intentions of the local church which celebrates the sacraments or of the Christians who receive them.

If we compare this pastoral situation with the praxis of the catechumenate in the second to fourth centuries, some startling contrasts emerge. The appreciation of initiation in this period, as the root experience for all other sacramental celebration was demonstrated in very practical ways. The lengthy catechumenal period was essentially a process of clarification of intentions, as we shall see in the next section. The celebration of the Word of God and the individual rituals which marked the progress of the catechumen revolved around the cross and resurrection of

Christ, as God's meaning challenging the meanings that candidates gave their own lived experience.

These early initiating Christian communities were well aware of how the commitment of their members would be tested both in intermittent persecutions and in the daily life of the Roman Empire. The catechumenate's function, then, was to teach a doctrine to be lived so that the proclamation and mission of the believing community, in turn, would be credible to the people of its time.

The success of the catechumenate in this two hundred year period, from a pastoral viewpoint, is extraordinary. Certainly the number of martyrs who witnessed to the death even as catechumens is impressive. Less dramatic but equally remarkable is the rapid evangelization of this period carried on by the committed baptized and catechumens. Finally, there is the incalculable effect of such shared commitment on the life of the Christian community whose rites of passage helped them to reappropriate old commitments and to move on to new ones.

For the contemporary Church the question of Christian commitment is equally pressing. The ways in which we initiate Christians or help them appropriate that same commitment at a later period deeply affects the praxis of all the other sacraments for which initiation is the root and model. The ways in which the celebration of any sacrament permits Christians either to escape from or to deepen their commitment to God's meanings and Christ's cross has a pervasive impact on the quality and credibility of a particular Christian community's witness to the Gospel. We will now examine how the symbolizing community challenges and evokes such commitment in the rites of the catechumenate process.

The Symbolizing Community

Rituals of commitment do not exist in a vacuum. Rather, as argued earlier, the rites of passage only have their full impact within a community which interacts and changes with the candidates so that the resulting communal fabric is renewed and strengthened. In the long run, the decisive test of rites of passage is the renewed commitment to the community. Rosabeth Moss Kanter captures this larger vision of commitment: "The search for community is also a quest for direction and purpose in a collective anchoring of the individual life. Investment of self in a community, acceptance of its authority and willingness to support its values is dependent in part on the extent to which group life can offer identity, personal meaning, and the opportunity to grow in terms of standards and guiding principles that the member feels are expressive of his own inner being. Commitment to community norms and values, or moral commitment, involves securing a person's positive evaluating orientations, redefining his sense of values and priorities so that he considers the system's demands right and just in terms of his self-identity and supporting the group's authority becomes a moral necessity."[9]

The rituals of the RCIA will be inevitably misunderstood, and thus misused, if the contexts for this sacramental process are ignored. In other words, the staged ritualization of conversion that is the RCIA assumes its full potential only when celebrated within a committing community. The ministries of such a community reflect and symbolize the commitment demanded of both baptized and candidates in the various catechumenal rituals. In the following sections, then, we will examine: (1) how the community uses these rituals to evoke commitment; (2) how the catechumenal ministries enable both baptized and candidates to enter into this process of commitment; (3) how catechumens appropriate the commitment meanings of the catechumenal rituals.

Communities of Commitment

The ecclesial community is not a passive audience watching candidates perform rituals. As Erving Goffman has eloquently argued, even such an apparently passive group of onlookers do influence the performance of ritual for better or worse.[10] Moreover, in the classical understanding of Tertullian or Augustine, the role of the initiating community is to "key" (to use Goffman's musical analogy) catechumenal rituals. "A keying, then, when there is one, performs a crucial role in determining what it is we think is really going on," as Goffman remarks.[11] The early Christian communities, for example, took oil or salt, methods of selection and election, and transformed the meanings of these ordinary objects and events.

Translated into our concerns, the Church community spells out the meaning of conversion to Christ by actively "doing the meanings" which it teaches. The Church cannot simply provide theories which explain rituals, but, rather, must relive with the candidates the experience of salvation which it proclaims. If there is one major reason for the dismal failure or the superficial implementation of the RICA, it is naive assumptions about the role of the local church in "begetting Christians," to use Augustine's telling phrase.

In brief, if we are to "key" the specific rituals of the RCIA, we must take seriously the remainder of the ritual's introduction: "The initiation of the catechumens takes place step by step *in the midst of the community* of the faithful. *Together with the catechumens*, the faithful reflect upon the value of the paschal mystery, renew their own conversion, and by their example lead the catechumens to obey the Holy Spirit more generously" (n. 4).

When the candidates, in response to the celebrant's question about what they are seeking from the Church, answer "Faith," the request is actually a startling one. Faith, understood as a committed response to God's offer of salvation, is mediated through the body of Christ, a local group of imperfect Christians called a "church." Later, in the celebrant's prayer, this theme is taken up again: "Today, *in the presence of your community*, they are answering your call to faith" (n. 82). This second statement complements the first. Faith is both the unearned gift of God and the enabled response of the individual who is strengthened by a core group of Christians.

Rather than vague references to the universal Church or even the local church, understood as a large anonymous diocese or parish, the first and most tangible expression of Church as enabler of conversion may be a more specific group of Christians such as the catechumenal team. This does not preclude a growing awareness of the union of all Christian communities or of the diocese as a local church, but helps focus the symbol and responsibility of begetting faith.

The Church's Understanding of Commitment

Implicitly weak ecclesiologies are learned in praxis when Church structures are offered as a substitute for a living Church community. The relation between the faith of the individual and that of the community then becomes a theological statement that seems to have no reference to the experience of either the candidate or the baptized. Therefore, it is important, as the RCIA notes, that the whole Christian community assembles for some catechumenal celebrations (n. 105), and that catechumens are gradually introduced into the worship of the whole community (n. 106). In this way, both the core support group of Christians and the larger community reflect the faith that commits Christians to God and one another at the same time.

For better or worse, the quality of faith-commitment in the local Christian community is mirrored in its practical expectations of catechumens. If the catechumenate, for example, is viewed as a more updated form of "instructions for converts," then this one-sided intellectual presentation of the faith can hardly be expected to substitute for the process of conversion. If practical concerns (for example, baptism in preparation for marriage, a catechumenate based on the school year, etc.) become the overriding and decisive factors in the implementation of the RCIA, then the community's conception of Gospel conversion and commitment may be faulty.

The community's notion of commitment is tested in practical terms of how long the catechumenal preparation should last. If the local community shares the same criterion as the RCIA— sufficient maturity in conversion and faith—then the suggestion of the rite that the catechumenate "may last for several years" (n. 98) will be taken seriously.

Finally, the sense of mission of the local Christian community is challenged when it invites catechumens to share in the work of the Gospel. When the celebrant explains, for example, the confirmation dimension of initiation as strength "to be active members of the Church and to build up the body of Christ in faith and love" (n. 229), or when the mystagogical period is seen as the "full and joyful insertion into the life of the community" (n. 235), the Church community's understanding of its mission is brought into sharp focus. Does the local parish, for example, have any Gospel work (for example, feeding the poor, care of the sick and elderly, etc.) to call either the baptized or the candidate to?

To summarize, the symbols and rituals of the RCIA assume their full meaning when a Christian community understands and celebrates them with a deepening sense of commitment. This ecclesial dimension is crucial because the catechumenal process is as necessary for the renewal of that community as it is for the preparation of its candidates. The success of renewing parishes and religious communities as neo-catechumenal communities in Europe is but one example of how this theory has been worked out in praxis.[12]

Celebrants of Commitment

The ministries which support and enable the catechumenal process are a second important context for the commitment of initiation and its celebration. Liturgical participation presupposes that both celebrants and participants bring to these rituals their own experience of what God has already done in their lives. Both baptized and candidates can only respond to Christ's sacramental presence with the free gift of their whole selves, as Vatican II so beautifully expressed it (*Constitution on Divine Revelation*, I, n. 5).

In addition, the special role of any sacramental ministry is to assist others to symbolize honestly so that they can participate fruitfully. The Church has always balanced its insistence that any sacramental action is grounded in Christ (and, therefore, not dependent on the merits of the minister) with its conviction that the role of the minister is to assist Christians in a knowing, active, and fruitful reception of a sacrament.

The primary ministers of the catechumenal process are all

those who have been called by the Church community to teach, guide, and celebrate with the candidates what God is doing in their lives. These ministers should become role-models of what they teach and celebrate with others. In a very real sense, the catechumenal team should represent a cross-section of the larger community. Like the early house-churches which were centers of Christian living, ministry, and hospitality, so catechumenal teams should symbolize the Christian commitment to which the rituals of the RCIA are continually referring.

The sponsor is an important example of one such ministry. The crucial role of sponsors is captured in the question of the celebrant in the introductory rites: "My brothers and sisters gathered here and you who present these candidates: are you ready to help them come to know and follow Christ?" (n. 77). To fulfill such a role, the sponsor must become a partner in the ongoing process of conversion. Not perfect but honest and aware Christians are required for such a ministry. They should be able to witness from their own spiritual autobiographies how the impact of the cross and the hope of the resurrection transform ordinary lives. By their active commitment to this service, sponsors exemplify the meaning and cost of mission within the Christian community.

Another important ministry is the celebration of the word of God throughout the whole process of the catechumenate. The sacramental presence of the word of God is, as we shall see in the next section, the major formative ritual of commitment that spans the whole catechumenal process. In the initial invitation of the community, the catechumen hears this challenge: "We welcome you into the church to share with us at the table of God's word" (n. 90).

The RCIA, in spelling out the anticipated goals of such celebrations, also indicates the tasks of its ministries. The first goal of celebrations of the word of God is "to implant *in their hearts* the teaching they are receiving" (n. 106a). The RCIA then goes on to give some examples: "the unique morality of the New Testament, the forgiving of injuries and insults, the meaning of sin and repentance, the duties Christians have to carry out in the world, and so on" (*ibid.*). In other words, constant encounter with the word of God should gradually transform attitudes, values, and life-styles. But this demanding process of commitment can only occur when catechumens are shown how to dialogue with their experience and to see how the word of God contests their interpretations of their actions, attitudes, and goals. The other gains of such celebrations, prayer and gradual insertion into the worship of the community, are tied to this same process. To minister the word of God, then, in the catechumenal process is to help clarify and call out new commitments of self-gift and service. There is, after all, no other way to learn to be like Christ (Rom 6:4–5).

Commitment always entails moving beyond where we are in terms of our service and vision. But, as noted earlier in R.M. Kanter's remarks, such commitment is usually evoked within certain types of communities. In the next section, we will comment briefly on some ritual examples of how the RCIA ritualizes these dimensions of shared commitment. Our present concern has been to show how the minister's and the catechumenal team's attitudes about these rituals will inevitably key catechumenal celebrations and participations in them.

In these rituals, the ministers witness to the ways in which Christ purifies and strengthens each one for a unique service of the Gospel. This ministry should not be done from an impersonal or detached position but rather as a result of interacting with the candidates in the celebration of the Word of God. Perfunctory ministry of these rituals, on the other hand, teaches an incorrect doctrine about God's presence and our response in commitment. In brief, the classical axiom, "the law of worship is the law of belief," is demonstrated, for better or worse, by the minister's own awareness and attitudes and their impact on the catechumenal participants.

Rituals of Commitments

Rituals, at their best, are like keys which unlock the meanings and commitments that participants are called to. This ritual effectiveness is linked to the cultural resonances of certain actions and words. As has been often pointed out, the catechumenal rituals were culturally derived, for example, from the bathing habits of the time, the anointings used in sports and medicine, the branding of servants and soldiers, and the myriad actions of everyday social intercourse.[13]

These cultural connections also suggest some of the pastoral problems in using such rituals. If the catechumenal rites of laying on hands and anointing, for example, are not as obvious in their meaning to a twentieth century candidate as they would have been to a third century person, then communication of meaning may be impeded. As Raymond Firth notes, "communication is the test of a symbol that survives."[14] In analyzing the commitment dimension of the catechumenal rituals, it is important, then, to remember the crucial roles of the community and its ministries. The pivotal question is not whether anointing with oil of itself, for example, communicates a certain meaning, but whether the ecclesial and ministerial contexts assist the catechumen in appropriating the meaning of the act.[15]

Turning to the rituals themselves, we find a major scriptural symbol of commitment in the introductory rite: "You have *followed* his light. Now the way of the Gospel opens before you.... You are called *to walk* by the light of Christ.... This is *the way of faith* on which Christ will lovingly guide you to eternal life. Are you ready to *enter on this path* under the leadership of Christ?" (n. 76).

The above text uses a privileged scriptural metaphor for choice and commitment—"the way." Contemporaries of Isaiah had no problem in understanding his urging: "... while from behind, a voice shall sound in your ears: *'This is the way; walk in it,'* when you would turn to the right or to the left" (Is 30:21). To "walk" images the way one lives, chooses, commits oneself. In the New Testament, the Letter to the Ephesians, in particular, favors this metaphor. Although English translations sometimes select the word "live," the Greek verb (*peripateō*) is more powerful: "I plead with you, then, as a prisoner for the Lord, *to walk worthy* of the calling to which you have been called.... You must no longer *walk* as the pagans do" (Eph 4:1, 17).

If we were to translate this teaching of Ephesians into contemporary language, we might say: "Buy into God's vision of life and its purpose, and thus become Christian." Even in these introductory rites, candidates are being asked to make certain commitments just as earlier candidates in the community of Hippolytus in third century Rome were asked to demonstrate their seriousness by their willingness to give up certain jobs which compromised Gospel values (*The Apostolic Tradition*, 16). Equally important is the fact that not only must the candidates reply to this challenge, but the celebrant then asks the community if they are ready to help the catechumens (n. 77). The response, "We are," is the local church's commitment to the process of "begetting" Christians.

It is not by chance that the sign of the cross marks the beginning of each Christian celebration. As noted earlier, this ritual signing symbolizes the focal point of Pauline teaching: the cross of Christ as the source of salvation. In the first reception of this treasured symbol, the connection between "the Christian way," discussed above, and the sign of the cross is made: "Please come forward, together with your sponsors, to receive the sign of your new way of life" (n. 83). Whether only the forehead or other parts of the body are signed, the message is the same: "May these catechumens take up their cross, live always by its saving power and reveal it in their lives" (n. 87). For Christians who make the sign of the cross often enough but are no longer challenged by its meaning, participation in this ritual can be a powerful reminder of forgotten truths.

The Word of God as Commitment

One major obstacle to perceiving the celebration of the word of God as an act of commitment is the attitude of many Christians. The theological theory of Vatican II once again spoke of the word of God as presence: "He (Christ) is present in his word, since it is he himself who speaks when the Holy Scriptures are read in the church" (*Constitution on the Sacred Liturgy*, n. 7). But in pastoral practice this is sometimes difficult to experience when the Scriptures are proclaimed poorly or in a perfunctory fashion, when the responsorial chants seem nothing more than a test of memory, and the word of God is explained in boring, irrelevant, or even inadequate ways.

As argued earlier, the word of God is our guide on the path of conversion. The word calls us back to the words of our own story and reveals the importance of our conflicts and crises, at each stage of our lives for shaping new commitments that will be needed. When the catechumen is first given the book of the Gospels, the accompanying charge is a challenge to live, and not simply read them: "Receive the Gospel, the good news of Jesus Christ, the Son of God" (n. 93). For these celebrations of the Word of God to have their full impact, the community and its catechumenal team will have to rethink the role of the participants. In this regard, the current RCIA is of little help since it pre-supposes that the liturgy of the word will be done effectively, an assumption that is pastorally naive.

Commitment must be invited from participants if rituals are to have their full impact. Applying this principle to the celebrations of the word of God, there should be a significant place for both meditative silence and some sharing about the import of the readings for the experience of the catechumen. Finally, there should be the possibility for some spontaneous prayer which flows from this exchange. The suggested prayer over the catechumens after this celebration of the word of God contains a comment which sums up the complexity of this task: "These catechumens, our brothers and sisters, have already *traveled a long road*" (n. 94). The word of God helps catechumens retrace their steps along that same road so that they may begin to rediscover how values and choices of the past shape the present.

If commitment to the Gospel way is to be evoked, then the meanings and lessons drawn from that long experience must be progressively and effectively clarified by the word of God. One of the concerns of the early catechumenates was, as J. Berntsen has argued, "the shaping of religious emotions and affections in the context of teaching doctrine."[16] In other words, Gospel commitment must be grounded in the total experience of the catechumen. The continuing celebration of the word of God is a privileged space and time for this wholistic Christian formation.

The scope of this article does not permit an extended analysis of the remaining catechumenal rituals in terms of commitment.[17] R.M. Kanter's observations serve as a guide to such a project: "Group involvement is often conveyed through rituals in which the whole unit participates symbolically affirming the commitment to their joint endeavor. These rituals both express and reinforce jointly-held values and represent ways of coming together as a group, of feeling closer to one another."[18] Whether we look at the texts for blessing of the oil of catechumens ("Bring them to a deeper understanding of the Gospel, help them to accept the challenge of Christian living"—n. 207), to the formal renunciation of "Satan and all his works" (n. 217), to the charge given with the lighted candle ("Walk always as children of the light"—n. 226), and so on, the language and rituals of commitment are to be found throughout all the stages of the RCIA.

Summary

To an earlier group of faltering candidates and baptized, the writer of the Letter to the Hebrews issued this challenging call to commitment: ". . . let us draw near in utter sincerity and absolute confidence, our hearts sprinkled clean from the evil which lay on our conscience and our bodies washed in pure water. Let us hold unswervingly to our profession which gives us hope, for he who made the promise deserves our trust" (Heb 10:22–23). For almost two thousand years, communities of Christians have been trying to respond to that challenge.

In our own day, we are fortunate to have once more a pastoral process for forming Christians and reforming, at the same time, the baptized. The heart of this process is conversion. But such conversion always entails our old and new commitments to God's meanings and Christ's self-gift. This is, indeed, the promised strength of the Holy Spirit which "will make you more like Christ, and help you to be witnesses to his suffering, death and resurrection. It will strengthen you to be active members of the Church and to build up the body of Christ in faith and love" (n. 229).

Notes

1. See D. Borobio, "The 'Four Sacraments' of Popular Religiosity: A Critique," *Liturgy and Human Passage*. Concilium 112, D. Power and L. Maldonado, eds. (New York: Seabury, 1979), pp. 85–97.

2. V. Turner, *The Ritual Process* (Chicago: Aldine, 1969); *idem*, "Passages, Margins and Poverty: Religious Symbols of Communitas," *Worship* 46 (1972) 390–412, 482–94; here, 402–03; A. Pasquier, "Initiation and Society," *Structures of Initiation in Crisis*. Concilium 122, L. Maldonado and D. Power, eds. (New York: Seabury, 1979), pp. 3–13.

3. R. Duffy, *Real Presence. Worship, Sacraments, and Commitment* (San Francisco: Harper and Row, 1982), pp. 112–114; henceforth, *Real Presence.*

4. W.A. Meeks, *The First Urban Christians. The Social World of the Apostle Paul* (New Haven: Yale, 1983), p. 89, though notice Meek's reservations about how aware Paul's readers were of this usage.

5. *Ibid*, pp. 74–110.

6. I have treated this at greater length in *Real Presence*, pp. 32–57.

7. *On Penitence*, 6. Here I use W. LeSaint's translation in *Tertullian. Treatises on Penance* (Westminster, Md.: Newman, 1959), p. 26

8. See R. Duffy, "Formative Experience and Intentional Liturgy," *Studies in Formative Spirituality* 3 (1982) 351–61.

9. *Commitment and Community. Communes and Utopias in Sociological Perspective* (Cambridge, Mass.: Harvard University, 1972), p. 73.

10. *Frame Analysis* (New York: Harper and Row, 1974), pp. 124–31, 540–41.

11. *Ibid*, p. 45

12. See G. Zevini, "The Christian Initiation of Adults into the Neo-Catechumenal Community," *Structures of Initiation in Crisis* (cf. n. 2), pp. 65–74.

13. See A. Scheer, "The Influence of Culture on the Liturgy

as Shown in the History of the Christian Initiation Rite," *Structures of Initiation in Crisis* (cf. n. 2), pp. 14–25, esp. 16.

14. *Symbols Public and Private* (Ithaca: Cornell University, 1973), p. 34.

15. See M. Douglas, *Natural Symbols. Explorations in Cosmology* (New York: Pantheon, 1970), pp. 1–18.

16. "Christian Affections and the Catechumenate," *Worship* 52 (1978) 194–210.

17. I will propose an extended analysis of these rituals in a forthcoming book *The Challenge of Initiation,* scheduled for publication by Harper and Row in late 1984.

18. Kanter, *op. cit.,* p. 47.

Dynamics of Conversion

Edward K. Braxton

I. Introduction

It is significant that the revised rites of Christian initiation did not come at the beginning of liturgical reform but rather after the Church had been involved in nearly a decade of liturgical renewal. For this reason the RCIA manifests a greater appreciation of the far-reaching nature of liturgical reform and clearly expresses a renewed pastoral orientation. In the case of initiation a clear distinction has been made between the "initiation" of adults and the "baptism" of children. There are now two separate rites with separate general instructions. In the adult rite, baptism is the climactic moment in the larger initiation process. The instruction for the adult rite begins by acknowledging that the spiritual journey of adults is very diverse and marked by discernible stages. There is the point of initial conversion in which a person expresses his or her desire to become a Christian and is accepted as a catechumen. This is followed by a prolonged preparation period, during which the catechumen's faith is allowed to grow to maturity. Finally, there is the actual reception of the three sacraments of initiation, baptism, confirmation, and Eucharist.

This stage structure of the RICA is marked by a strong but non-explicit awareness of the developmental dynamic of human growth, maturity, and commitment. The pioneering work of researchers such as Jean Piaget, Lawrence Kohlberg, and Erik Erikson has been translated by James Fowler into a model of faith development that supports the stage structure of the new ritual. Other essays in this collection treat this material in more detail. In light of this stress on growth and process, it might be helpful to examine the dynamic nature of faith before concentrating our attention on the issue of conversion.

II. The Dynamic Nature of Faith

What really do we mean by faith? We often hear such expressions as: "Keep the faith." "Practice the faith." "Don't lose your faith." "They have fallen away from the faith." What precisely are we talking about when we say this?

Is faith, in its most fundamental form, the intellectual acceptance of a body of teachings about: the existence of God; Father, Son and Spirit; the content of revelation; the truth of Scripture; the purpose of the Catholic Church; the essence of the priesthood; the importance of the sacraments; the limits of ecumenism; the extent of the role of women in the Church; the reality of sin and grace; the nature of hell, purgatory and heaven?

Does one automatically have faith by intellectually affirming propositions about these matters? Some would answer "yes" without hesitation. Not only do they consider these propositions to be the contents of faith, but also they would go so far as to take certain Aristotelian-Thomistic expressions of these propositions and even the rather simple question and answer format of the Baltimore Catechism to be the ageless and *exclusive* expression of "the faith." Thus, from this perspective Christian initiation is the rather simple matter of accepting "the faith."

There is a sense in which this is partially true. Clearly the elaboration of beliefs about these ancient Christian concerns is closely related to faith. Through them faith is expressed, specified and even embodied. However, the example and teaching of Christ, the evidence of Scripture and tradition, the witness of holy women and holy men, and the best of Catholic spirituality and theology strongly attest to the fact that faith, in its fundamental form, is a far more dynamic, existential and personal reality than is conveyed by a somewhat static, propositional and theoretical listing of theological ideas, religious images, Church doctrines or Catholic beliefs.

The fundamental reality of faith is the radical personal and communal response to the unconditional gift of love that the Creator has for each of us. It is this essential movement of divine life in us that is mediated by the words and symbols of faith, but this spiritual reality is prior to and deeper than our religious words and symbols. Thus "the faith" can never be adequately thematized or verbalized in public discourse. This is why the Church has not only creeds, doctrines and, hopefully, challenging homilies, but also stained glass windows, deeply moving ceremonies, a rich musical heritage, the rhapsodic expressions of mystics, and a radical social commitment. Thus faith is a response of the whole person—mind and heart. Faith is the on-going and lifelong response to the call to conversion that is now whispered and now shouted in the depths of a person's very being, and in the unraveling history of a family, a community, a nation and the whole Church. Thus, when the potential new Christian signs the book of election, he or she is not signing a contract for membership in a "church." Rather it is a commitment to struggling to take up a new way of life.

Faith, then, is a response to the call to conversion. Conversion is one of those words that has an odd sound in Catholic circles. We usually do not use the word when speaking about ourselves. We use it when we speak of coming forward for Christ at a Billy Graham rally. Conversion is what happens to Christians of other traditions when they become Catholics! But I am using conversion in a sense that applies to us as much as anyone else.

Conversion is the transformation of the way we experience ourselves, others, the world and the universe. In Nietzsche's phrase, conversion is the "transvaluation of values." Those who undergo conversion shall never be the same again. They are turned inside out and upside down by God's Holy Spirit. They are Abram—asked to sacrifice his only son Isaac—become Abraham; Moses before the bush that burns but is not consumed; Saul—knocked from the horse—become Paul; a young Jewish peasant girl become Mary, the mother of Jesus, because of her startled "fiat" to the angel's call. They are Simon—prancing in the waves of a stormy sea—become Peter; and perhaps even Jesus of Nazareth triumphing over desert temptations—as the Father's Christ.

In every human person the reality of conversion is a complex of on-going, overlapping elements. The dynamics of the spiritual pilgrimage of those being instructed into the Christian faith may be viewed as several different, but related, forms of conversion.

Bernard Lonergan has offered a systematic framework in which to understand this phenomenon. Conversion, he suggests, operates on many different levels within the human person. It may be religious, Christian, ecclesial, moral or intellectual. The pages that follow give a very simple summary of the approach taken by Lonergan in his analysis of the conversion experience. As we reflect upon each of these elements or forms of conversion, it is important to keep in mind that the distinctions are logical ones that make the whole process easier to grasp. However, separation for the sake of analysis should in no way suggest that each "form" of conversion is a separate reality in a person's life and not related to the next "form" of conversion.

III. Religious Conversion

Religious conversion comes about as one becomes aware of what Karl Rahner aptly terms "holy mystery." It is palpable realization of the religious dimension at the ground of all human experience and activity. Religious conversion is a deeply embedded sense of the holy or the sacred. It is a tacit awareness of the absolute meaning, purpose and graciousness of one's own life and the entire universe. A potentially mature Christian may be under the sway of this religious conversion even when he or she is questioning or doubting particular teachings or practices of the Catholic Church. It is possible to be religious in this primal sense and be indifferent to or even in opposition to some aspects of institutional religion. Similarly, it is possible to be an active and seemingly faithful member of institutional religion and be devoid of this primal religious awareness. Institutional and ideological loyalty do not automatically constitute religious conversion. Nor do they automatically constitute faith. Such loyalty, devoid of spiritual vitality, is but the simulation of faith. A grasp of this distinction is very important for those who are guiding catechumens.

As we grow in this fundamental awareness, we gradually grasp the source of our experience of "holy mystery" as not some impersonal energy or blind force but as an intelligent, loving, even personal reality. Thus we can speak of God. Through the power of this divine spark at the center of our being, we grasp that life is not so much sound and fury signifying nothing, not a tale told by an idiot.

In spite of the inscrutable paradoxes and seeming tragedies in personal, communal, and world history, conversion to God yields the affirmation of the complete intelligibility hidden in the riddle of life. Within this hope-filled horizon prayer enters our lives, and we make our own way with John of the Cross in the ascent to Mount Carmel, with St. Teresa of Avila through the rooms of the Interior Castle and with Thomas Merton up the Seven Storey Mountain. This is obviously not a simple matter. New members of the people of God must be taught how to pray by their sponsors, how to approach the Sacred Mystery with an awareness that they walk on holy ground.

IV. Christian Conversion

Christian conversion consists mainly in the new believers' response to the question Jesus put to Simon and the disciples: "Who are people saying that the son of man is?" In Christian conversion we recognize in the life, ministry, teaching, death and resurrection of Jesus the presence of the Father's Christ— and thus in Christ you have what Edward Schillebeeckx has appropriately called the sacrament of the encounter with God, Emmanuel, God with us. Christian conversion, however, is not automatic. It is not the sure result of attending all the sessions of the parish RCIA program. Christian conversion, in its initial expression, is not in the main a matter of theological theories about humanity and divinity in Jesus or metaphysical constructs about the Trinity.

A person may come to Christ without knowing anything

about the great Christological speculations of Nicaea and Chalcedon. Christian conversion is a personal appropriation of the paschal mystery. Jesus becomes not a stained glass window figure, not a holy card image, not an emasculated statue on a pedestal, not a coherent doctrine, but a living, pulsating, challenging brother and Lord who walks with you and talks with you and tells you that he loves you. Christian conversion is, as St. Paul says, "to put on Christ." It is to answer Jesus' question ("Who are people saying that the son of man is?") with your whole being, "You are Christ, the Messiah, the Son of the Blessed One." The ability of already initiated members of the faith community to witness to the centrality of Christ in their lives is of critical importance for those who are just beginning to follow the Way. This can be problematic in some Catholic communities where Christian faith is a very private matter and parishioners are uncomfortable speaking about their faith in Christ to others.

V. Ecclesial Conversion

Ecclesial conversion is the turn to community. It is joining with others in hearing the word, breaking the bread and blessing the cup. When we are really converted to the Church we realize that religion is not just a matter of "Jesus and me." Under the influence of ecclesial conversion we embrace a living tradition, a community and world family in which there are different ministries and the special responsibilities of the bishops and the Holy Father. Ecclesial conversion is not so much having faith in the Church as it is the response to the empowering Spirit's call to *be* the Church, to assemble as the "ecclesia," the people of God. What we believe in is the Creator Father revealed in the Redeemer Son by the Power of the Spirit. If Christ is the sacrament of the encounter with God, then the Church is the sacrament of the encounter with Christ, and every Christian is called to be the sacrament of the encounter with the Church.

In our day, of course, new members of the Catholic family of faith must be given a special sensitivity to the ecclesial nature of other Christian traditions and the growing movement toward unity. Confidence in the truth of Catholic Christianity should not imply a rejection of all that is good in other traditions. Thus, there should be no more talk among new Catholics about "non-Catholics." After all no one will call them a "non-Orthodox," "non-Anglican," or "non-Lutheran."

Avery Dulles in *Models of the Church* and *A Church To Believe In* reminds us that there are many ways of looking at the mystery of the Church. Besides various positive images of the Church as herald, sacrament, servant, mystical communion, and community of disciples, it is possible for a Christian to have an incorrect or at least inadequate model of the Church. Some may conceive of the Church according to a military metaphor with strict rank and control, or as a defensive bastion of a peculiar ideology. Nor should the Church be conceived of as an "elevator," a heavenly transport system, that takes us to our "spiritual" destination. We cannot crowd into the Church the way we crowd into an elevator, indifferent to and even suspicious of those around us. If we do, when we get to the top, the divine elevator conductor may well declare: "It was the way you treated one another on the trip up that counted. So, down you go!"

VI. Moral Conversion

Moral conversion is the effort that those to be reborn by water and the Holy Spirit must make to respond to the call of God in conscience. It is the quest for authenticity in every aspect of one's life. Like Thomas More, Dorothy Day, Mother Teresa, Dr. Martin Luther King, Jr. and Archbishop Romero, the morally converted person seeks out the good, and does the good simply because it is the good. The morally converted person cares not for appearances, rewards, punishments, advancements or fleeting public opinion. He or she has gone beyond Kohlberg's five stages of moral development to his sixth stage: the grasp of transcendent values. The morally converted man or woman strives to conform the deeds incarnated in his or her life with the values inscribed in his or her heart. In the effort to achieve moral conversion one struggles with St. Paul, who said to the Romans, "That which I know I should not do, I do, and that which I know I should do, I do not do."

Priests, deacons, religious and lay leaders who accompany catechumens in their journey of faith must make it clear that the authentically Christian understanding of moral conversion embraces far more than the sixth and ninth commandments. As important as these matters are, moral conversion is not simply a matter of sexuality, birth control or abortion. Moral conversion encompasses every personal and public area of human thought and conduct where Gospel values are at stake. Thus every new Christian who wishes to live out the meaning of their faith must scrutinize, from a Christian perspective, his or her attitudes, actions and omissions in many areas: war and peace, government, social justice (e.g., racism, sexism), care for the environment, just wages for workers and the horrible prospect of nuclear holocaust. It is well for those adults preparing to be baptized to be reminded that as they grow in faith and the moral life, luxurious living quarters, extravagant vacations, an excess of material goods, irresponsible use of alcohol, smoking, indulging one's appetites, overeating, and not exercising and caring for one's health are all instances of moral decline and potential sin. They are not simply minor bad habits that are the unavoidable by-products of American secular culture.

VII. Intellectual Conversion

Intellectual conversion is the slow and painful process through which the thinking person experiences the liberation and integration of the mind. By means of intellectual conversion the thoughtful new member of the household of faith comes to terms with the complexity of the world and the eros of the mind to know everything about everything. It is the realization that things may not be the way they appear. This paper appears to be a solid mass, but in fact it is a mass of moving particles. Knowing is more than seeing and touching. It appears that the sun rises and sets. But it does not. The earth turns on its axis and moves in an elliptical circle around the sun.

Future Christians should not be burdened with tired old battles between religion and science. If they are encouraged to be open to intellectual conversion they will recognize that there is no one exclusive path to truth: poetry, proverbs, music, art, and common sense can all direct one to the true. The findings of serious studies in history, psychology, anthropology, philosophy, science and theology are not necessarily in conflict. By a certain intellectual agility one can appreciate their complementarity. Usually where conflict arises, e.g., so-called creationist vs. evolution conflict, it is because of the inexact use of language, the presence of bias, misinformation, or issues which simply are not mature.

The seemingly irreconcilable conflicts between Galileo and the Church in a past age are easily reconciled today because a higher viewpoint makes it possible to see that positions that seemed in conflict were actually the result of the confusion of scientific and theological categories. Sometimes it is a matter of just plain error as Pope John Paul II seems to have acknowledged in the case of Galileo and the Spanish Inquisition. Intellectual conversion integrates all forms of human knowing and understanding in a dynamic synthesis. Those who join the Church should be encouraged to seek God's truth wherever it may be found. Where faith is deep and strong there should be no fear that it shall be easily undone.

Those who come to Christ need not be startled when biblical scholars tell us that the infancy narratives may be a special literary form, and not literal accounts of the birth of the Messiah. Literally speaking, there may have been no shooting stars, singing angels, or exotic magi. But the fundamental theology of the uniqueness of Christ conveyed by the infancy narrative is, and remains, ever true. The same may be true of the creation story in the Book of Genesis. The account of the seven days of creation may convey timeless religious truths through a literary form, but the literary form may convey implausible cosmology. The general direction of Charles Darwin's theories of natural selection and the origin of the species may be better science than Genesis. After all, Genesis is not a science book. But responsible science does not undermine the religious vision of the creation story any more than responsible theology undermines the legitimate advances of science. Without intellectual conversion, many religious people cannot live with this dialectical view of reality.

Intellectual conversion reaches its zenith when the person of faith recognizes his or her own intellectual limitations in the face of the absolute mystery of God who dwells in unapproachable light. Due to the limits of language, the historicity of the human race and the permanence of mystery, intellectual conversion must fight arrogance and gnosticism and yield to the light of the Holy Spirit if we are to experience the paradoxical enlightenment that the anonymous medieval mystic termed as the entry into "the Cloud of Unknowing."

VIII. Conclusion

Thus the on-going conversion that feeds the life of faith of the catechumens and of all Christians is manifold. It is religious—the turn to the holy; Christian—the turn to Jesus as the Christ; ecclesial—the turn to community; moral—the turn to values; and intellectual—the turn to a wholistic understanding of truth and human wisdom. Obviously, conversion does not operate with a predictable mechanical sequence. One does not necessarily move smoothly from religious conversion to intellectual conversion—from the day of election to the celebration of baptism, confirmation and Eucharist. The whole process overlaps and compenetrates. Thus in a particular catechumenal or Christian community there may exist a very strong loyalty to the Church—a manifestation of ecclesial conversion—but there may be little or no religious sense, or there may be a highly devotional commitment to Jesus as the Sacred Heart—but one so exclusive and privatized as to all but exclude the community (hence an absence of adequate ecclesial and moral conversion). Again a new adult Christian may have a highly refined sensitivity to fundamental moral values—authentic moral conversion—but due to certain radically negative experiences and intellectual questions, he or she may have times when agnostic or even atheistic thoughts seem to surface, thus calling into question religious conversion. This whole process is very different from person to person. Ethnic, racial, educational, cultural and emotional factors all impinge significantly to give a particular shape to each individual's journey. An artificial uniformity should never be imposed simply in order to get everyone baptized at the Easter vigil. The Christian journey is on-going; it does not end on Holy Saturday.

It might be helpful for those directing the program of the adult catechumenate to reflect and pray about their own faith journey. In what way is conversion absent or present in their particular life of faith? What have been the particularly difficult and challenging aspects of growing into a mature faith? What were the most beneficial activities and resources of the faith community that assisted them in times of doubt, difficulty and frustration?

It would be equally wise to reflect upon the whole parish community insofar as this is possible. How effectively has the parish adapted to the renewal of the Second Vatican Council? What is the quality of liturgy, preaching and pastoral care in the parish? What organizations or movements in the parish are particularly vital and reflect a real response to the call of the Holy Spirit? Which ones are simply there because they have always been there?

In such a reflection it might also be possible to become better aware of some of the more outstanding examples of growth in Christian faith in the parish. Perhaps some of these men and women could be called upon to pray with the catechumens and share their own experiences of conversion.

Obviously, to be effective a parish catechumenate program must be well planned and well organized. But this does not mean that it should be structured to the point of rigidity. If the growth in ecclesial identity is as dynamic as has been suggested, then it is inappropriate to hope for uniform results. In some cases timetables will have to be adjusted. In others a great deal of follow-up will be needed. In still others the program may have to be greatly simplified in order to have any real impact upon the participants.

All of this will take much time, energy, and resources when many of our parishes are understaffed and suffering a decline in resources. Eventually it may mean focusing more of our pastoral energy upon the adult members of our parish families. Where we are able to make the commitment and build upon the potential of the new Rite, I have no doubt that new and old members of the Church will be enriched and, as a result, an important foundation will be laid for the shape of the Church to come.

Sociological Perspectives on Conversion

Robert D. Duggan

Introduction

Our Catholic tradition has always insisted that the mysterious workings of divine grace do not operate in ways that run contrary to our humanity. The famous adage of medieval theologians, "Grace builds on nature," is but one expression of this long-standing realization that we are called to divine love in a manner that is profoundly respectful of who we are as human persons. This insight in turn seems rooted in our basic faith in the incarnation: ours is a God who has embraced our humanity in the fullest possible way, and that embrace has meant salvation for all that is human.

The conversion experience is perhaps the most dramatic example we have of the intersection of divine and human trajectories. Nowhere else does divine grace appear so mysterious and ineffable, nor can one find any better example of the rich intricacy of human experience. Little wonder, then, that this phenomenon has exerted so powerful an attraction on students of human behavior, as well as theologians.

The present essay is an attempt to share the perspective of social scientists as they explore the human contours of the conversion experience. We shall look at what experts in the sociology of religion have said about the human factors which contribute to religious conversion. We do this with an eye to discovering what is most relevant in these studies for the implementation of the Rite of Christian Initiation of Adults. The sociological viewpoint we shall examine is admittedly a limited one. Unlike theology, it claims no access to divine truth. Indeed, careful scientists in every field today are quick to point out the limitations of the data which they present. And those whose view are represented in this essay would be the first to caution the reader that their research is valid only to the extent that it is based on what can be empirically verified.

One result of this constraint is that the sociological study of conversion almost invariably equates conversion with a change in institutional affiliation. What is most easily observable is whether or not an individual "belongs" to a particular religious group, and how completely that belonging manifests itself through various external behaviors. The scientific literature *never* claims anything with regard to the secrets of the heart, the hidden truth which is known only to God and the individual believer. Hence, it is entirely possible that someone could go through all of the motions of conversion from a sociological perspective (change of professed belief, altered lifestyle, new worship patterns, etc.), and still remain sinful, unbelieving and hypocritical. Nonetheless, such a theoretical possibility remains the exception, and few people would hold that this invalidates the whole enterprise. Indeed, the level of sophistication possible with the social scientific tools used today is quite impressive. Factors to measure even the degree of religious commitment are often incorporated into studies, and it seems reasonable to assume a *general* correspondence between the sociological understanding of conversion as affiliation and some sort of interior movement of a spiritual or religious nature. This, in fact, is our premise, based on that Catholic tradition of incarnational faith mentioned above: careful scientific study of religious conversion will tell us something about how God's grace works in and through our human experience. And, the more we can find out about how conversion "works," humanly speaking, the better able we should be to implement the RCIA in a way that is respectful of God's designs as well.

A few ideas by way of background should help to introduce the reader to the world of contemporary studies in the sociology of religion. The last twenty-five years have witnessed among sociologists a growing interest in religious behavior as an object of study. With this increased interest has come an increased precision and development of the science. The phenomenal growth of the "new religions" during the decade of the 1970's focused particular attention on the conversion experience as a pivotal question. In the past fifteen years especially, there has been an increasing number of studies attempting to understand and explain the social forces at work behind individual and mass conversion experiences to these groups. Although most of this research has been done on smaller religious groups—what Ernst Troeltsch called a *sect* as opposed to a *church*—we believe that much of value can be learned from them for our own situation. A number of social scientists have done research which indicates that the findings on conversion drawn from studies of sects have applicability for those in larger churches as well.

Conversion Typologies

Two broad approaches have dominated this research: conversion typologies and studies of the process of conversion. The first of these continues the approach begun by the early psychologists of religion (William James, Edwin Starbuck, J.B. Pratt, etc.) whose efforts were directed primarily at categorizing the "types" of conversions which they observed. Frequently suggested were such categories as sudden/gradual, conscious/unconscious, intellectual/moral/social, and so forth. Many contemporary sociologists continue along this same line, attempting to identify significant features which characterize various kinds of conversions, and then studying carefully the variables involved in each kind. No consensus has been reached on which categories are most useful; and, needless to say, there are nearly as many typologies suggested as there are researchers. But there have been recent efforts to put together these many different approaches and find the categories that seem to be most helpful.

We can summarize much of this material by citing what has been suggested as six major "motifs" which give to conversion experiences their predominant characteristics.[1] These six categories are all aspects of a highly complex experience. They have been selected because they happen to be those which are most frequently stressed in reports by individuals who have undergone religious conversion.

1. Intellectual Conversion. This describes the experience of those who come to embrace a new religion primarily through an individual process of investigation. There is usually little or no external social pressure involved, and the subject's search usually extends over a number of months or even years. Typically, there is only moderate emotional arousal on the part of the convert, and significant levels of belief seem to precede actual participation in the organization's rituals or other activities.

2. Mystical Conversion. The classic model for this kind of conversion is the Damascus road experience in the life of St. Paul. Coherent, logical terms seem unable to capture the intensity and richness of the event which is described as overtaking and overwhelming the individual. A period of stress is sometimes noted beforehand, but the critical moment is usually quite brief and often occurs with a virtual absence of social pressure. High levels of emotional arousal are reported, and the experience generally signals the beginning of belief and participation in the ritual and organizational activities of the religion involved.

3. Experimental Conversion. This expression describes a process of transformation which occurs in situations with little social pressure and low level emotional arousal, where prospective converts "try out" the new religion's beliefs, attitudes and behaviors in tentative fashion first, and only gradually make the commitment to belong. Basically a form of socialization into a new community, this kind of experience uses what has been called "situational adjustment" or "commitment mechanisms" to secure change in the individual. Such conversions follow the general pattern by which any new social role is learned, as assimilation into a new group occurs.

4. Affectional Conversion. This form of conversion has been the object of intensive study since it was highlighted in a very influential article by John Lofland and Rodney Stark in 1965.[2] In it the formation of strong interpersonal bonds with someone already within a religious group is seen as crucial in the process of conversion to that group. More will be said below about these conversion experiences in which affective ties play a decisive role; but we note in passing that the cognitive element is de-emphasized, social pressure is present mainly as support and attraction, and only moderate emotional arousal is present. The process involved is relatively prolonged, and as in experimental conversion, belief follows from organizational involvement rather than precedes it.

5. Revivalist Conversion. This expression identifies the familiar pattern associated with profound religious transformation which occurs within the context of a highly charged group experience. The social pressure of group "contagion" produces a short-term, intensely felt emotional experience which may compress a range of feelings from guilt and fear to joy and ecstatic release. As in the previous two types, participation in the group's rituals and activities usually precedes belief.

6. Coercive Conversion. The final pattern of conversion is associated with the phenomena described in "brainwashing" or "mind-control" experiences and, some would add, in many of the cults that flourished in the 1970's. An extremely high degree of external pressure over a long period of time is seen to produce intense fear and uncertainty, which then "flips" over to empathetic identification and even love. This is an admittedly rare form of experience, but its high visibility in the last decade has resulted in considerable literature on the subject.

The sixfold typology of conversion outlined above is but one of several available in current sociological literature. It was constructed by looking at only five variables (degree of social pressure, duration, level of affective arousal, affective content, belief/participation sequence). Many other variables could be included to construct different typologies, and the literature offers numerous examples of such efforts. We have chosen this one because it is fairly representative and suggests the broad range of experience which can underlie religious transformation. It also makes quite evident the reason why it is possible to find widely divergent definitions of conversion among social scientists who study the phenomena. Usually only the most generic definition, such as "a process of changing a sense of root reality,"[3] can claim general acceptance. This diversity should make us cautious in our own generalizations about the conversion experience which is the aim of the RCIA. Not surprisingly, people come to their God in nearly as many different ways as there are people, and we shall discuss later some of the implications this holds for catechumenal formation.

Process Models of Conversion

We mentioned above that two main approaches have dominated in contemporary studies of the conversion experience. The first of these we have described as an effort to construct a typology of conversion. The second approach is marked by the attempt to study and describe the *process* by which conversion occurs. We have already touched on some of these efforts in our discussion of typologies, but now we shall examine more closely several which have been particularly influential and seem most promising for our purposes.

In the early 1960's Lofland and Stark studied a tiny sect they identified as the "Divine Precepts Cult." (It has subsequently been established that this group was the Unification

Church of Reverend Moon.) As a result of their study, they proposed a seven-step model which they said described the process through which individuals passed in becoming "converts." Theirs is what is called a "value added" model. In other words, there is a kind of funneling effect including psychological, situational and interactional factors which govern who actually converts, with each new condition increasing the probability that conversion will occur. In brief, they suggest that for conversion people must (1) experience enduring, acutely felt tensions (2) within a religious problem-solving perspective (3) which leads them to define themselves as religious seekers, (4) encountering the cult at a turning point in their life (5) wherein an affective bond is formed (or pre-exists) with one or more converts, (6) where extra-cult attachments are absent or neutralized, and (7) where if they are to become deployable agents, they are exposed to intensive interaction.

This proposal has proven a rich and stimulating one, and much of the subsequent literature has been concerned with validating or refuting, refining or expanding it. We will indicate very briefly the tenor of the critique which has emerged. The general applicability of the first three factors, identified as "predisposing conditions," has been called into question. Research has been done in which one or all of these factors could not be verified to any significant degree among the "converts" studied. On the other hand, the argument is made that pre-dispositional factors can be found so widely in the general population that their identification among converts does not really move forward one's theoretical understanding of conversion. For example, nearly everyone at some time experiences "acutely felt tensions" in life, sometimes with relative frequency, so that it can seem meaningless to speak of this as a "pre-disposing factor" for conversion. While the experts continue to debate which specific factors, if any, are likely to function as pre-dispositions, it is at least helpful for us to be aware of the possibility that prospective converts may be found in higher proportion among selected populations with particular characteristics.

The remaining four conditions of the Lofland-Stark model, called situational factors, have also been the subject of careful critique. Factors four and six (turning point and absence of external ties) have been called into question by more than one study. This is not to deny that either of these could ever be a contributing factor to conversion experiences. The opposite is clearly the case. But it does lead to caution about accepting them as *necessary* conditions in the "conversion careers" present in a given group. In this regard, subsequent research has shown that the nature of the religion in question (its organizational structure, its status in the larger society, etc.) is a highly significant variable. The final two situational factors proposed by Lofland-Stark (affective bonds and intensive interactions) have consistently emerged in the literature as extremely important in the conversion process, and we shall explore them more at length below.

Another contribution made by those reacting to the Lofland-Stark model is worth mentioning. It has become increasingly clear that autobiographical conversion accounts must be approached with considerable circumspection. Conversion involves a reconstruction of one's past, and in the account of that experience there is frequently injected a new "meaning system" which effectively changes the interpretation of previous events. One's "old" past and one's "new" past often bear slight resemblance to each other. The story which the convert tells must be heard as part of a present effort to maintain, or even provoke, the conversion being described as past event. The formative power of such discourse ought not to be underestimated, and this bears attention by all involved with catechumens.

A concern increasingly voiced today is that much of the sociological literature on conversion presumes that an individual is simply the product of social forces, a passive figure drawn away from one position and into another by influences over which little control can be exercised. Admittedly there is a degree of this sort of mechanistic bias evident in the Lofland-Stark and other studies. Recently, however, the convert is more and more seen as an actively strategizing "seeker" who exercises substantial freedom and control over his or her situation. The more dynamic, interactionist models which permit such a view are obviously more easily reconciled with the understandings operative in the RCIA. But both approaches have something to offer. The passivist paradigm has shed considerable light on the social forces which work on many individuals in the process of religious change. As long as one avoids a simplistic cause-effect understanding of how these forces operate, much helpful information can be gleaned from these studies. The activist paradigm, however, provides an important balance by stressing the manner in which individuals exploit groups and social forces in a self-determining effort at creating and maintaining meaning in their lives. From this perspective, conversion is seen as part of a range of religious phenomena which are both a personal and a collective accomplishment. In addition, conversion is seen as an on-going effort rather than a "terminal act."[4] The convert continues to strategize in order to make the conversion take root in daily life, thus making conversion an "emergent" or "evolutionary" reality. It is in living out the converted life that conversion is in fact "accomplished." Here the similarities are striking with Catholic thought on "continuing conversion" as it is expressed in the theology of the Rite of Penance and in the RCIA.

Lofland-Stark's description of conversion as "coming to accept the opinion of one's friends"[5] sums up remarkably well what has proven most valuable in their study. Conversion is increasingly presented in the literature as a process of coming to see that reality is what one's friends claim it to be. The new self of the convert is defined in terms of the reference group that is being joined. In this context, affective bonds and intensive interaction assume tremendous importance. Rudy and Greil have suggested that in view of this importance, the question to ask is not about the exact nature of the conversion process, but how organizations should be structured to facilitate these bonds and this kind of interaction.[6] Their contribution to this focus has appeared in a series of papers studying groups called "sociological cocoons" or "organizations for the transformation of identity," such as Alcoholics Anonymous or various therapeutic drug communities. By looking at the operation of these highly successful groups whose explicit aim is "conversion" from one perspective to a radically different one, Rudy and Greil suggest that the more specific case of religious transformation can be better understood. Here we can only summarize briefly their major points.[7]

They begin by affirming that the central dynamic in the process of identity transformation is the shift referred to above in which one comes to see self and world from the perspective of a new reference group. In order to achieve this, successful organizations offer various mechanisms which protect prospective "converts" from sustained interaction with those who might discredit the new perspective being offered. This mechanism is often referred to as "encapsulation," and it may be physical, social or ideological. Physical encapsulation is found, for example, in a therapeutic drug community whose residential treatment center is in a remote area. Social encapsulation is effectively achieved by AA with its 90/90 rule, by which participants are expected to attend ninety meetings in as many days. Compliance effectively limits one's contacts with non-members during the period in question. Ideological encapsulation is more subtle, but frequently just as effective. This occurs when subjects are given an interpretive framework for dealing with "outsiders" which insures against real challenge to the position of the group, as when all who contest the validity of a dogmatic position are judged to be under the influence of evil spirits.

Rudy and Greil point out also that the extent to which coercion is involved in a situation constitutes a crucial variable. Where it is present to any real degree, great energy must be expended in discrediting the previous identity (unfreezing) before a new one can be instilled. The presence of a power-dependence relationship is also an important factor in the sociological cocoon. Those who have some measure of control over one's basic needs will the more readily influence one's view of reality. Hence, the greater the degree of dependence of a member on the organization, the easier it will be to effect change. Related to this, and to encapsulation, is the characteristic by which a group is known as a "greedy organization." That is, total allegiance is demanded, and the organization is not content with claiming only a segment of an individual's energies. Finally, organizations for the transformation of identity must make use of various commitment mechanisms whose aim is to lead the individual to see his or her interests as identical with those of the group. Because of the value of this factor for our purposes, we will look at commitment mechanisms more carefully below. For the present, we note that in summing up their understanding of conversion, Rudy and Greil have stated, "In our view, these processes are essentially the same. Conversion *is* commitment."[8]

In looking at the structures by which successful organizations operate as sociological cocoons, we do not suggest that the RCIA ought to become such an organization. However, there seem to be valuable insights available here about how an individual can be brought to a new sense of identity through the affective bonds which are formed in the catechumenate and the intensive interaction which occurs within that primary reference group. Below, we will explore further what implications this holds for the catechumenal experience.

Commitment Mechanisms

We have alluded to the relevance of studies on commitment for our understanding of religious conversion. In this connection, the work of R.M. Kanter,[9] stands out as particularly helpful. Kanter has studied a variety of utopian societies to determine what factors can be identified that contribute to the willingness of members to invest energy and loyalty in such an organization. She has identified six general organizational strategies and structural arrangements, which she calls "commitment mechanisms," that seem significant in this regard. The value of understanding how these mechanisms work should be apparent for all concerned with helping people to take the steps necessary for full initiation into the Church via the RCIA. She puts the mechanisms into three pairs, corresponding to three areas she considers essential for group survival: *continuation of membership, group cohesion,* and *social control.*

Continuation of Membership

1. *Sacrifice.* This first mechanism, related to a member's continuance in an organization, suggests that the decision to give up something considered valuable or pleasurable in order to belong to a group tends to motivate one to remain within that group. This is based on the simple insight that the more it "costs" an individual to belong, the more "valuable" will membership seem, and the more one will be willing to make the necessary expenditures to maintain that belonging. Examples of the kind of sacrifice a group might demand of members range from various forms of abstinence (oral, sexual, etc.) to a variety of austerity measures (voluntary poverty, primitive living conditions, etc.). Membership is perceived as even more sacred and meaningful when the sacrificial step is conceptualized as an act of consecration that brings one closer to God.

2. *Investment.* This second commitment mechanism which heightens motivation for continuance in membership does so by giving an individual a stake in the success of the group. When one commits present as well as potential future profits to a group, there is a natural urge to remain as a participant in order to realize those profits. This can be accomplished by requiring new members to turn over their property or money to the organization, or simply by requiring a substantial investment of time and energy with only a promise of future reward. The tendency, of course, is to remain active in order to realize the fruits of that investment. If the investment is irreversible (e.g., property actually signed over, or an official policy of "no refunds" to defectors), then the impact of the investment is correspondingly greater. Associated with this mechanism is the making of what is called "side bets," the unanticipated and often intangible investment of resources that

occurs once a person is a member. For example, once one's personal reputation becomes linked to that of the organization, the likelihood of withdrawal or disengagement is significantly lowered.

Group Cohesion

3. *Renunciation.* The second area of concern relative to an organization's survival is what Kanter calls group cohesion. In order to secure this cohesion, a group must attach an individual's fund of affectivity and emotion to the group. Renunciation involves giving up competing relationships outside the communal group, as well as individualistic, exclusive attachments within. Separation from outsiders, what we called encapsulation earlier in this chapter, can be achieved not only by physical separation, but also by developing a special jargon, by wearing distinctive dress that sets one apart, and so forth. Renunciation of individualistic or exclusive ties within the group can be enforced by celibacy, compulsory "free love," or lesser forms of control over members' association patterns. The results of all such mechanisms is a heightened emotional attachment to the group itself.

4. *Communion.* Closely related to renunciation is this mechanism whereby members are brought into meaningful contact with the collective whole, so as to experience oneness with the group and develop a "we feeling." Group cohesion requires a strong sense of fellowship which in turn gives members determination to continue in the face of obstacles. This can be accomplished by an experience of persecution, facing collective problems, or by more positive steps that build homogeneity and overcome individuality. Examples would be sharing of goods in common, communal

dwelling or dining arrangements, and especially participation in group rituals.

Social Control

5. *Mortification.* The third and final area mentioned by
Kanter as significant for organizational survival is
termed social control. The object of this area is commitment to group norms, i.e., an individual's acceptance that the organization's demands are right, and
that obedience to its authority is a moral necessity. The
first mechanism which works to achieve this is called
mortification, whereby private states are submitted to
social control and a former identity is exchanged for
one defined by the community. These processes emphasize the individual's smallness before the organization's greatness and aim to convince the member of his
or her insignificance without the guidance and meaning given by the group. In addition, a new set of crite-
ria is given for self-evaluation and self-criticism,
insuring that only the model offered by the group is
judged acceptable. Countless strategies are available to
achieve this end: public confession, mutual criticism,
spiritual stratification which rewards "success" (defined according to group norms), various punitive measures for infractions, and so forth. The common
denominator in these mechanisms is that they all strip
away certain aspects of an individual's identity, foster
dependence on authority for direction, and substitute a
self which is susceptible to the influence of the group.

6. *Transcendence.* The second commitment mechanism
aiming at social control is called transcendence or surrender. This occurs when an individual attaches his or
her decision-making prerogative to a power greater
than self, surrendering to the higher meaning contained by the group and submitting to something be-

yond the self. In order for this to take place, personal identity must be fused with the group to such an extent that carrying out the demands of the organization becomes a moral necessity. Specific processes that achieve this end include various mechanisms which create what Kanter calls "institutional awe." For example, the group is elevated to the level of the sacred, its mastery over human existence is indicated by a pervasive philosophy or minute regulation of all behavior, or authority in the organization is surrounded by mystery and placed at a distance from ordinary members. Transcendence is also accomplished by requiring ideological conversion for membership, as when special vows must be taken for membership or when faith is tested to insure legitimacy of membership. Finally, tradition is seen as a transcendence mechanism whereby the appeal to what is hallowed on the basis of its ancient lineage calls for surrender on the part of the member.

Each of these six commitment mechanisms that have been identified by Kanter can and do give rise to many more specific strategies. Each in its own way contributes to reinforcing the commitment that a member has made to belong to a group. It is possible in discussing such mechanisms to receive the impression that they take away an individual's freedom to choose. That is not at all the case. Like the other social forces at work in conversion, these can help to reinforce personal decisions, but they do not deny the radical freedom which remains at the heart of any choice regarding participation in a religious movement. Our intent is to develop a better feel for how we can support and strengthen the journey of those who have chosen to seek God through the structures and processes offered in the RCIA.

Conversion to Catholicism

Our survey of sociological studies of conversion would be incomplete if it failed to mention the important work of Dean Hoge.[10] In what he terms "a study of religious change among

Catholics," Hoge sets out to look at a representative sample of those entering and leaving the Catholic Church, to see who they are and what reasons can be determined for their changed religious affiliations. The theoretical model which he offers in describing conversion to Catholicism is a simplified version of the studies we have already seen. He proposes three conditions, or decision points, in the process of becoming a Catholic convert. With his data he suggests that these three conditions describe the path followed by the majority of converts to the Catholic Church in America today.

The first condition is that the person have a Christian world view. Very few persons without this religious perspective convert to Catholicism in our culture. The second condition calls for the individual to have at least a minimal felt need for spiritual life or Church involvement (or a change in these if they are already present). To these two pre-disposing factors, Hoge adds the condition that the person develop an affective bond with someone within the Church who provides a "facilitating relationship" for entry into the Church. By now the reader will find all of Hoge's points familiar. He breaks no new ground, but it is most helpful to have him replicate for the Catholic Church important data on conversion which generally has come from studies of much smaller sects.

In addition to his proposal regarding the process involved in conversion to Catholicism, Hoge also provides some very helpful information on who the converts have been in recent years. In effect, Hoge's study embraces both major trends in contemporary conversion studies: a process model and a typology. His typology, like his process model, is relatively simple. Of the conversion stories studied by him, ninety-five percent of the converts can be classified in one of these categories: *intermarriage converts, family life converts, seeker converts.*

Intermarriage converts were a significant group in the sample of two hundred and ten converts studied, with thirty-eight percent in this category. Hoge classifies in this group persons who are already or about-to-be married to a Catholic, and who feel some concern for the marriage or are influenced by their spouses and relatives in their choice of religion. Frequently a secondary motivation, such as personal problems, spiritual need, and so forth will also be present.

Family life converts are the second type identified in Hoge's study, and they are numerically the largest group, comprising forty-five percent of the sample. In this category are persons with children being raised Catholic, and who express concern over the children's religious upbringing. Like the earlier type, family life converts frequently have secondary motivating factors in addition to this primary one.

Seeker converts are the last type and also the smallest at twelve percent of the sample. These are persons motivated by a spiritual search or a sense of void or meaninglessness in their lives. Interestingly, this is the kind of convert that most social scientific research has focused on in the past.

The role of relationships with persons already within the Church should be noted in all of Hoge's types. He makes special mention, as have other researchers, of how important a factor this is in making a potential convert into an actual convert. All of the "pre-disposing factors" imaginable may be found in a given individual, but it is the presence of a particular person(s) with whom that individual can interact that seems to make the crucial difference in so many cases. In the dry jargon of the social scientists, "affective bonds" and "intensive interaction" emerge consistently as key factors in the conversion process. What this means in human terms is that our search for God is inevitably made easier when we find someone(s) who can incarnate for us personally the love for which we all yearn.

Implications for the RCIA

It is time now to shift our attention from the carefully measured statements of the sociological researchers, and to try to make explicit some of the implications which this data holds for those who minister to the conversion experience within the context of the RICA. Our focus at this point becomes that of pastoral theology, an interdisciplinary approach that attempts to bring theological truth to bear on the understandings we have uncovered of how the human side of our encounter with God actually works. Our insights will be suggestive rather than programmatic, since any first efforts at building bridges between separate disciplines are of necessity tentative. But the exciting aspect of our project is the fresh look at our catechumenal experiences that is made possible by the juxtaposition of these two previously unrelated perspectives.

We begin by affirming the basic value of a social scientific approach to conversion, despite its obvious limitations. The renewed sacramental theology from which flows the RCIA sees human experience as the locus of our encounter with God, and for this reason it treats seriously the phenomena which social scientists help us to examine at close range. The sociological perspective has also helped us to appreciate more keenly the ecclesiological framework within which conversion is viewed in the Rite. The oft-quoted phrase, "the initiation of catechumens takes place step by step in the midst of the community of the faithful" (#4), takes on new significance in light of the powerful social forces that we have discovered to be at work in an individual's decision to join a new religious group. The theological understanding of initiation as incorporation into the ecclesial body of Christ is faith's way of stating the deeper dimensions of human religious belonging.

Conversion, then, in both perspectives is understood to be the result of individual and social factors, or, as it has been called, a "personal and collective accomplishment." These polarities which were sharpened above in the formulation of the "passivist paradigm" and the "activist paradigm" receive balanced attention in the vision of the RCIA. The pastoral challenge is to implement the Rite in such a way that that balance is maintained. Emphasis on personal decision and response to God's call should be present in every catechumenal experience. Enormous attention can be appropriately given to the effort of helping candidates discern what steps they should be taking on their unique spiritual journey. But this always needs to happen in the context of a community that is encouraging, guiding, even leading the way. As the Rite of Election so eloquently states, it is the

Church who calls. Conversion is a gift of grace mediated to a particular individual through a particular community, and both dimensions must receive their proper attention.

Recent sociological literature has focused on the question of what sort of organizations tend to foster commitment. We think that this is a healthy pastoral approach for local parishes as well. The question should be asked more often: How can we be the kind of community that "facilitates" those who are seeking conversion? The sociological distinction between recruitment, affiliation and maintenance reminds us that there is a threefold task for the parish community: evangelization, ministry to the conversion experience, and helping to support the commitment of all who are already members. Identifying what structures and what organizational strategies will best do this should be a top priority on the agenda of every pastoral leadership team.

This effort will involve a more intentional approach to all of the groups to which a local catechumenate is open. The work done on conversion typologies can remind all of us how diverse are the ways to God. Our catechumenal structures would make a tragic mistake if they simply replaced the old "convert classes" with some new "packages" that forced everyone into the same mold. Outreach programs of the parish evangelization team need to be carefully targeted. Dean Hoge's data has given helpful pointers to groups which will be "ripe" for a carefully formulated overture. Selected mailings to non-Catholic spouses and non-Catholic parents of children in the parish religious education program, events aimed at helping "seekers" ask their questions and tell their stories, all of these and more are approaches that look to the particularity of selected populations within a parish and seek to respect the uniqueness of the conversion journey that is theirs. Similarly, once a group of catechumens is assembled, the diversity that inevitably is present must be reflected in formation experiences that allow for individual needs. Catechists should see themselves as resource persons who help candidates develop their own "learning packages," rather than as instructors who give everyone in the class the same information.

A more differentiated approach to the formation process

will also allow greater flexibility in terms of the time-frame for catechumenal experiences. We are rapidly overcoming the "program" mentality which put catechumenates on a tight schedule, thank God. Scientific studies can reassure us now that for some people a longer period of testing is necessary than for others, and this has nothing at all to do with bad faith or resistance to grace. The RCIA's vision always included a respect for the gradual nature of conversion (e.g., its decision to incorporate "stages" into the process), but many parish "programs" have had to rediscover this obvious but forgotten truth.

The recent effort in many catechumenal experiences to help candidates "tell their story" is a development that seems very wise in light of our sociological data. We have seen that conversion accounts play an important role in *constructing* the conversion which is being described as past event. In addition, the categories used in that narrative play a crucial role in the interpretive task of finding meaning in one's life journey. These insights remind us of the importance of giving candidates an adequate language with which to describe their experiences. Here, the function of Sacred Scripture is essential. The worldview of biblical faith is the basic stance which we seek to give to new members. Groome's shared praxis approach to storytelling[11] is solidly based because it allows one to read into one's own experience the faith vision that makes a Christian. Because it is richly symbolic, the language of Scripture also tends to be more "open" and hence more accessible to persons of every background than might be the case with the particular theological terminology of our dogmatic formulations.

Heavy exposure to Scripture throughout the catechumenal experience has yet another basis to recommend it in the sociological literature. The famous definition of Lofland-Stark that conversion is coming to accept the opinion of one's friends makes a good case for extra efforts to make certain that one's "friends" who guide the catechumenal formation process are steeped in Scripture. For the most part, world-views are shared unintentionally, by attitudes and actions rather than by the carefully prepared lessons we teach. This means it is crucial that we surround those undergoing a conversion process with people who have "put on the mind of Christ Jesus" and whose every approach to life is rooted in the faith of the Gospels.

This seems the appropriate place to discuss two factors which we have seen emerge consistently as of primary importance in the conversion process: affective bonds and intensive interaction. The wisdom of the RCIA in restoring the role of sponsor to a place of importance in the catechumenal experience should be apparent by now. Persons may have every "pre-disposition" possible, they may be "seekers" for months and even years, but it is only when a "facilitating relationship" allows them to connect with a particular community that religious conversion seems to come to fruition. Those with experience in catechumenates are unanimous in affirming the importance of the sponsor. Nothing is quite as powerful as that one-to-one experience of being loved as an individual, feeling the strength and support of affective bonds that deepen and grow, and coming to understand that all this is connected to a particular community which makes such an experience possible. Practically speaking, this suggests the value of putting considerable institutional energy into developing a group of persons available to perform this ministry. The very best persons should be selected for this role, and training, encouragement and enabling resources should be made available so that they can do the best possible job. Other bonds will form with various members of the community, of course, and this too must be fostered by the pastoral leadership team. Most simply, the social scientists are reminding us that when we love people deeply, they will respond with love; and—the theologians would add—thus do they come to know the love of God.

This insight is the basis for the second factor which has received so much attention in the literature: the importance of intensive interaction. We would certainly not recommend making catechumenates into sociological cocoons. But at the same time we need to appreciate the strength and support offered by a closely knit network of persons who meet regularly to provide help during the conversion process. Increasing segments of the Church are discovering the potential of base communities as change agents in people's lives. In a sense, every catechumenate should be that kind of an experience for the candidate who seeks membership through community. Extreme forms of encapsulation would be contrary to the pluralistic spirit which is such a proud part of our Catholic heritage. But at the same time, there are human needs for reinforcement of a new identity which can only be met by procedures that involve leaving behind a previous way of life for the sake of something new. Unless a new set of demands is made by our catechumenal experiences, full conversion may not happen as readily. It is of course possible to go too far, to become a "greedy organization" that makes excessive claims. But our recent Catholic experience has certainly not erred in this direction. Too often, we have asked too little, called for a conversion that is faint at best, and discovered that "something more" is usually demanded, and catechumenal expectations have been shaped accordingly.

A group that opts for intensive interaction among its members quickly recognizes the need to employ various forms of the commitment mechanisms which we have mentioned above. Our Catholic tradition already has a highly developed sensitivity to these techniques as a result of centuries of experience with them in the novitiates and other formation experiences of our religious orders. A whole literature of ascetical training and spiritual development exists in which these mechanisms are presented as part of a coherent vision of "life in Christ." We need to make more intentional use of this practical wisdom that is still part of our living tradition. Catechumens need to be taught the spiritual value of sacrifice, seen as a way to a closer union with God. They need to be asked, gradually but progressively, to make "side bets" which invest them in the Church with an eye to the future as the only place where that investment is adequately returned. Spiritual direction must be provided for every candidate, and the pastor of souls should be prepared to deal sensitively with questions such as which relationships or entanglements in a person's life have to be renounced in order for conversion to go forward. Catechumens must be part of a special group, and they should come to know their specialness through ritual moments that make indelible impressions. Dismissal of the catechumens from the Sunday Eucharist suddenly makes great sense when for the first time the neophytes are allowed to remain (and themselves bring forward the offerings) and *finally experience* what it means to "belong." Similarly, the wearing of white robes during mystagogia may seem to some a bit of liturgical antiquarianism, but watch what it does to reinforce that new identity which until now has only been talked about!

The commitment mechanisms which Kanter describes as operating in the area of social control are grouped under the headings of mortification and transcendence. The descriptions of both of these should have been recognized by anyone familiar with traditional approaches to spiritual formation in the Catholic Church. We have, as has already been mentioned, a highly developed repertoire of these strategies in our seminaries and religious orders. In suggesting the viability of drawing on this experience for the formation of catechumens, a word of caution must be expressed. In fact, this caveat might well be given concerning the entire sociological approach to conversion which we have been discussing.

Our caution is a reminder that the factors which induce conformity do not necessarily provoke conversion. Social pressure can be a two-edged sword. For beginners who are weak and in need of support, it can be a help toward conversion for the catechumenal process to employ consciously the strategies discussed above. But a closed and rigid religious system can suppress that freedom which is the authentic ground of the Spirit's work. In the post-Vatican II era a number of Catholic religious groups moved away from many of their traditional "commitment mechanisms" because they recognized that there was too much conformity and too little conversion being produced in their members. In some cases this realization brought too many changes too quickly, and an agonizing reappraisal was subsequently forced upon certain communities. Out of that experience we seem now to have reached a more mature and balanced approach to spiritual formation. Today there appears a clearer consensus that attention must be given both to factors which shape a social identity and to the mysterious freedom which marks the journey of each individual. Catechumenates would do well to harvest this wisdom in utilizing commitment mechanisms, while at the same time constantly appealing to the heart of the candidate whose response must be one of freely given love.

This caution is even more timely in view of the questionable nature of some of the "religious conversion" experiences which have received widespread publicity in recent years. The "snapping" phenomenon has raised the specter of mind-control and produced militant deprogrammers committed to undoing the damage done to those they consider helpless victims. The excesses are obvious on both sides, but the furor serves to remind us how delicate must be our approach to persons with whom we minister in our catechumenates. The great challenge we face is to respect the gentle ways of a God who confronts but never coerces, who leads but never manipulates, who invites but never demands, who supports but always allows us to journey in freedom.

The sociological perspective that we have shared asks of us the courage to look with a fresh and open mind at the mystery of religious awakening. This will require creative response on our part. We must shape catechumenal experiences which allow God's call to have its fullest possible impact on our lives and in our programs. The more we learn about how to minister to the human transformations which our catechumens undergo, the more we will be drawn to marvel at how truly mysterious are the workings of divine grace.

Notes

1. John Lofland and Norman Skonovd, "Conversion Motifs," *Journal for the Scientific Study of Religion* 20 (1981) 373–385.

2. John Lofland and Rodney Stark, "Becoming a World-Saver: A Theory of Conversion to a Deviant Perspective," *American Sociological Review* 30 (1965) 863–874.

3. Max Heirich, "Change of Heart: A Test of Some Widely Held Theories about Religious Conversion," *American Journal of Sociology* 83 (1977) 653–680.

4. Roger A. Straus, "Religious Conversion as a Personal and Collective Accomplishment," *Sociological Analysis* 40 (1979) 158–165.

5. Lofland and Stark, 871.

6. Arthur L. Greil and David R. Rudy, "What Do We Know about the Conversion Process?" unpublished paper (n.d.) 20.

7. Arthur L. Greil and David R. Rudy, "Sociological Cocoons: Organizations for the Transformation of Identity," unpublished paper (n.d.).

8. Greil and Rudy, "What Do We Know?" 17.

9. Rosabeth Moss Kanter, *Commitment and Community: Communes and Utopias in Sociological Perspective*, Cambridge: Harvard University Press, 1972.

10. Dean R. Hoge, *Converts Dropouts Returnees: A Study of Religious Change among Catholics*, Washington, D.C.: USCC, 1981.

11. Thomas H. Groome, *Christian Religious Education: Sharing Our Story and Vision*, San Francisco: Harper & Row, 1980.

Faith Development and Conversion in the Catechumenate

Romney M. Moseley

Introduction

Faith is a root metaphor that expresses the human quest for ultimate meaning. It is the activity of surrendering one's self totally to an ultimate and transcendent source of meaning and power. In religious terms, the heart is given completely to God, and this is precisely what is meant by the word *credo*—a compound of the Latin words *cor* (heart) and *do* (I give). The cognate verb to believe, a derivative of the German word *vorlieben* (to fall in love), also expresses what is meant by the word faith. Unfortunately, the dynamic and intimate connotations of belief and faith have been eroded by the more impersonal and abstract interpretations of these terms as assent to the truth claims of doctrines and sacred texts.

In the past decade or so, James Fowler's theory of faith development has been instrumental in refocusing our attention on the dynamic and interpersonal structure of faith.[1] Drawing on Jean Piaget's cognitive-developmental structuralism[2] and Erik Erikson's psychosocial theory of human development,[3] Fowler has proposed a conceptual framework for examining the cognitive and affective processes underlying our meaning-making activities throughout the life cycle. Fowler maintains that faith is a generic process that is common to all persons, and that it is not merely a phenomenon that is the property of particular religious groups and traditions. His chief theological ally for this position is the historian of religions, Wilfred Cantwell Smith, who defines religion as "a cumulative tradition" through which faith is culturally expressed. In contrast, Smith argues that faith is etymologically understood as the total surrender of the self to the transcendent.[4] Fowler is also strongly influenced by H. Richard Niebuhr's theology of radical monotheistic faith. Niebuhr's insistence upon the sovereignty of the One who is the ultimate source of meaning and value more so than Smith's penchant for etymological consistency is decisive in the shaping of the final goal (*telos*) of faith development. Accordingly, it is at stage six, the final stage of faith development, that the *telos* assumes a distinctively ethical form as *praxis*, i.e., actions that are undertaken in submission to the power of the transcendent One. Furthermore, it is also at stage six that the "eschatological proviso" of faith development is most evident.[5] Here we see life history as "enacted narrative,"[6] i.e., ultimate meaning as concretely realized through the ordering of our actual lived experience. Such pretensions to ultimate meaning are ultimately self-deceptive and are challenged by the eschatological promise of a future in which God's reign is ultimate reality. The elements of *telos* and *eschaton* therefore are of critical importance as we consider the relationship of faith development theory to the experience of conversion. These factors hold the key to what is essentially a religious theory of meaning-making, despite Fowler's insistence on preserving a structural distinction between faith and religion.

Stages of Faith Development

Let us turn then to a brief exposition of Fowler's six stages of faith development.

Stage One: Intuitive-Projective Faith

This stage is directly linked to biological maturation and to the acquisition of language. Cognitively, the young child (in the years through age six, approximately) is pre-operational in the Piagetian sense, i.e., he or she is unable to distinguish fantasy from concrete reality. Consequently, meaning-making is fantasy-filled, thinking is episodic, egocentric and one-dimensional. In other words, at stage one, dependence on the imagination is paramount as the child responds to the multitude of stimuli from the immediate environment.

Stage Two: Mythic-Literal Faith

This stage is marked by the beginnings of concrete operational thought. The ability to order the world through concepts of causality, space, and time is coupled with a fascination for narrative and story. The latter are comprehended literally and the child projects himself or herself into the fabric of the narrative. Play is enacted narrative. The nexus of interpersonal relations is widened beyond the immediate parental and familial environment to include peers and other authority figures. However, the person at this stage is unable to engage in mutual perspective-taking.

Stage Three: Synthetic-Conventional Faith

The hallmark of this stage is the structure of interpersonal relationships. A primary characteristic is the tendency to resolve disparate and conflicting aspects of reality by appealing to mutually shared feelings and conventional interpersonal virtues. The self that is constituted at this stage is a synthesis of perspectives held by significant persons. In effect, a conventionally acknowledged "generalized other," e.g., church, is tacitly maintained as the self's center of meaning and value. Stage three coincides with the transition from adolescence to adulthood, hence is found in both age groups.

Stage Four: Individuative-Reflective Faith

This stage is marked by a determined effort to evaluate the truth claims of ideological systems and a critical distancing from conventionally acknowledged sources of authority. The emergence of an autonomous self is coupled with a need to define the self in terms of personally selected ideas and values. This disembedding of the self from traditionally derived relationships may also be marked by a sense of commitment to self-chosen rules for governing relationships. The danger at stage four is ideological imperialism and fanaticism.

Stage Five: Paradoxical-Conjunctive Faith

Maintaining a pluralistic consciousness of reality without reductionism is the chief characteristic of this stage. Multiple meaning systems are held in tension in the interest of discovering a more inclusive truth which transcends the partial claims of any one perspective. A special characteristic of stage five is that it represents a cognitive-developmental stage beyond Piaget's stage of formal operations. This stage of "dialectical thinking" is supported philosophically by such figures as Husserl, Heidegger, Buber, Gadamer, and Tracy. Of particular significance is the hermeneutic idea of conversation as the process for reaching consensus on the meaning and truth disclosed in the religious classics. The person at stage five submits himself or herself to what David Tracy calls a "journey of intensification" into the "liberating paradox" of the particularity of his or her tradition and its claims of universality.[7] Consequently, there is a noticeable attentiveness at stage five to the power of the symbol and metaphor as these mediate the paradoxes of existence.

Stage Six: Universalizing Faith

Stage six espouses a normative vision of human development. As such, it is not empirically derived through interviews with subjects. It depicts the ultimate purpose or *telos* of human existence. The substance of this vision is derived from autobiographies and hagiographies of world transformers, for example, Martin Luther King, Jr., Gandhi, and Mother Teresa of Calcutta—persons whose lives have been shaped by paradigmatic manifestations or proclamations of what humanity is ultimately called to be. At stage six *telos* and *eschaton* are embodied in praxis—actions that are ends in themselves. These are emancipatory both in the sense of sacrifice of the self to the service of humanity and also in the sense of *kenosis*—the surrender of the self to the transcendent. Persons of this stage are "religious actualists"—that is, their lives are an event of apocalyptic transformation of self and world and a disclosure of the eschatological coming of the Kingdom of God.

Theoretical Considerations

At this point it is important to examine more closely the epistemological foundations of faith development theory.

The claim that stages five and six are cognitive-structural stages beyond stage four is highly debatable. One could argue convincingly that both stages five and six are simply differentiations in the *function* of abstract logical thought. This is precisely where Fowler's stages part company with Piaget's cognitive-structural stages. In fact, Fowler should have depended much less on Piaget's stages in formulating the progression of his own. Let us see then what Fowler has appropriated from cognitive-developmental structuralism.

In grounding his theory of faith development in Piagetian cognitive-structuralism, Fowler has adopted an epistemology which appeals to reason alone as the principle by which reality is ordered. Piaget is unmistakably Kantian in his emphasis on the knowing subjects' intrinsic capacity to impose meaning and order upon the datum of experience. What Kant referred to as *a priori* intuitions and categories of mind are reformulated by Piaget as genetic structures of cognition. The latter are evidenced by the development of knowledge along invariant and hierarchically ordered stages beginning with early sensory-motor experience in infancy, followed by pre-concrete operations and concrete operations in mid-childhood, and later in adolescence by formal operations or abstract logical thinking. The hallmark of Piaget's genetic epistemology is the claim that knowledge is constructed through the interaction of a knowing subject and the environment. Thus Piaget rejects rationalism, for example, Platonism, which denies the importance of sensory experience in the acquisition of knowledge and argues instead for the existence of innate ideas. This Piaget dismisses as "genesis without structure." Piaget also rejects classical empiricism, for example, the philosophy of Locke and Hume, as "structuralism without genesis." This position viewed the mind itself as the entity by which reality was ordered. Thus, the mind was conceived as a *tabula rasa*—a blank slate upon which sensory experience impressed its random complex of ideas. In mediating between these two epistemologies, Piaget opted for a cognitive-developmental structuralism in which the concept of structure defines the normative psychological operations governing the development of cognition. Basically, by structure is meant a system of internal relations with its own intrinsic self-regulating processes.

Accordingly, cognitive development involves the transformation of increasingly complex structures by means of which adaptation to the environment is made possible. Adaptation itself occurs along two lines, namely, assimilation and accommodation. Assimilation refers to the process by which data from the environment are incorporated by the available cognitive structures. Simply stated, without these structures, for example those governing the concept of causality, this information cannot be assimilated. Accommodation is the process by which cognitive structures are themselves transformed as data are assimilated from the environment.

What then is the heuristic value of Piagetian structuralism with regard to faith development? Studies by Elkind on the development of "religious understanding" from childhood through adolescence support the usefulness of Piaget's stages in identifying changes in religious meaning-making during the course of individual development.[8] Goldman (1964, 1965) has also found Piaget's stages helpful in gearing religious education to the child's cognitive abilities.[9] Both these researchers have not extended the concept of structure beyond the strictly cognitive operations. Nor have they hypothesized the existence of stages in adulthood that are qualitatively different from adolescent religious thinking.

A distinctive feature of Fowler's theory is that it postulates at least two post-formal operational stages in adulthood, namely, "dialectical thinking" at stage five, and "synthetic thinking" at stage six. The argument in favor of dialectical thinking is supported philosophically by Riegel[10] and empirically by Basseches.[11] This argument, however, is far from settled. Even more so is the hypothesis of synthetic thinking at stage six. For our purposes, it really does not matter whether there exists structurally identifiable post-formal operational stages. Of far greater importance is the concept of structure implicit in Fowler's stages. Here what we discover is an ambiguous mixture of Piagetian cognitive-structuralism, Erikson's passion for the intrinsic wholeness of the person, and Loevinger's [12] argument in favor of a principle of coherence underlying ego development.

An inevitable problem with Piagetian structuralism is Piaget's subordination of the affective to the cognitive. On the contrary, both Erikson and Loevinger maintain a more integrated approach to the dynamic interplay of the cognitive and the affective. Accordingly, we see Fowler implicitly opting for structure as a metaphor for internal coherence. As such, faith development is less concerned with the development of particular cognitive skills than with the construction of an integrated self. Moreover, whereas cognitive-structuralism is predicated upon the differentiation of *structure* and *content*, and conflates structure and *function*, Fowler's theory revolves around the differentiation of *structure* and *function*. Let me elaborate further.

The concept of Piagetian structuralism helps us to avoid the biases of cultural relativism by explaining differences in cognitive development on the basis of the evolution and transformation of biologically organized cognitive processes. The key factor here is the cognitive equilibrium achieved through the adaptative processes of assimilation and accommodation. Basically, cognitive development is predicated upon the ability to attain increasingly higher levels of equilibrium. It is precisely the principle of equilibrium rather than Piaget's stages, per se, that provides the connecting link between Piagetian structuralism and Fowler's theory of faith development.

The principle of equilibrium enables us to speak of a stage of cognitive or faith development. Basically, a stage is a specific form of equilibrium. In Piaget's theory, a stage is a "structured whole," i.e., it is an integrated system of cognitive operations which possesses a starting point as well as a point of termination. Stage transition is a result of dis-equilibration as new structures emerge in response to the activities of assimilation and accommodation. Each stage is a higher and more comprehensive level of equilibrium. In Fowler's theory, the concept of dynamic equilibrium is not restricted to the invariant functions of cognitive-structural integration and adaptation, but is defined in terms of the coherence of the self. Consequently, stage transition involves the disembedding of the self from its centers of meaning and value, and the adoption of qualitatively different strategies for organizing a coherent relationship to the world. However, Fowler does not address the issue of self-construction. Instead, he focuses on various functions of the self. For example, social perspective-taking, bounds of social awareness, form of world coherence, and locus of authority are viewed as structural aspects of a faith stage but they tell much more about the functioning of the self. The result is an ambiguous tension between an explicit neo-Kantian natural law theory of human development which emphasizes universal genetic patterns of meaning-making and a tacit neo-Hegelian emphasis on the historical maturation of a self. The former stresses self-regulatory or synchronic processes in human development; the latter poses an absolute transcendent Self as the guiding principle behind the evolution of the self. The self matures as it is shaped by knowledge of the absolute Self. It is in Fowler's sixth stage that we discover the most explicit example of this interplay of neo-Kantianism and neo-Hegelianism. On the one hand, this stage expresses a vision of the ultimate *telos* that we seek, namely, a universe that is shaped by moral principles upon which the very fabric of humanity rests, for example, justice and freedom. Without this *telos*, Fowler's stages of faith could be reduced to descriptive developmental psychology. On the other hand, stage six also articulates a neo-Hegelian transcendent and absolute Self that is the ultimate reference point of the embodied self. Mature faith is understood as the total surrender of the self to the Absolute; hence, the strong mystical character of stage six.

Erikson in his most recent book, *The Life Cycle Completed*, points out the irony in speaking of life as a cycle. Implicit is the notion of self-completion, but this is not to be undertsood as "a promise of an all-inclusive accounting of a perfect human life."[13] The same applies to faith development. Each stage of faith is a step toward a more coherent relationship to the One center of meaning and value. Each stage is normative; however, the norm is not simply established in *a priori* biological structures but is derived from the data of life history. And these life histories confirm that the self is constituted in relationship, not only to itself and the world, but also in relationship to the transcendent. What is described as stage six, therefore, is not an "all-inclusive accounting of a perfect human life" but a teleological and eschatological conception of the maturation of human relatedness to the transcendent.

Stages of Faith and Religious Conversion

In an earlier work, I distinguished two types of conversion on the basis of certain differences observed in converts to religious movements.[14] The distinction between content and structure in Fowler's theory provided the key to my typology of conversion. I discovered that there were persons, most of whom exhibited stage three faith, who converted from one religious movement to another. These conversions revolved around interpersonal relationships established with a significant person or persons in the group or denomination. These persons did not define their conversion to the group in terms of the truths held by the group, i.e., they were not ideologically committed. I termed such conversions *lateral conversions.* I applied the same term to conversions at stage four which were marked by a diffuse movement from one belief system to another in a protracted state of ideological confusion. In contrast to these intra-stadial lateral conversions, I reserved the term *structural conversion* to denote conversions that coincided with stage transition. This seemed to make sense at the time. However, with more sophisticated methods of analyzing interviews, it is evident that stage transition is far more complex and cannot be linked directly to conversion. Nevertheless, I see no reason to abandon the category of *intensification experiences* to denote ec-static experiences that accompany conversion. Such experiences are changes neither in content nor in structural stage.

There are several options available, including those suggest-ed by Fowler (viz., faith stage change without conversion; con-version without stage change; conversion that precipitates stage change; stage change that precipitates conversion; conversion that is concomitant with stage change; and conversion that in-hibits stage change).[15] In the absence of an empirical study of all the above, let me offer a theoretical alternative.

All the options mentioned, including lateral and structural conversion, are based upon the cognitive-structural distinction of structure and content. Having argued earlier that Fowler's concept of structures revolves around a principle of coherence governing human becoming rather than a principle of adapta-tion to the world, it is also appropriate to consider conversion from this perspective. The task at hand is to relate two dynamic and on-going processes, namely, conversion and faith develop-ment. Each embraces the self's relationship to itself, the world, and the Transcendent. It would seem that these processes are in-distinguishable. However, it is important to consider whether the concepts of *telos* and *eschaton* are also relevant to the process of conversion, and whether these concepts are identical with those in Fowler's theory. On this point, Bernard Lonergan's ty-pology of conversion is helpful.

According to Lonergan, three types of conversion may be identified, namely, intellectual, moral, and religious. The com-mon principle at work is the quest for self-transcendence. "It is to acquire the mastery of one's own house that is to be had only when one knows precisely what one is doing when one is know-ing." Moral conversion is "opting for the truly good."[16] It in-volves critical reflecting on the foundational values which give meaning to one's life. Religious conversion is the paradigmatic experience of grace. It is "falling in love" with "the ground of all self-transcendence" (*ibid.*).

Obviously, Lonergan's typology of conversion is not based on a stadial-developmental process. Nevertheless, since there is an implicit maturational principle at work, the question of teleology needs to be addressed. Lonergan is unmistakably Aristotelian. His typology of conversion is a naturalistic and organic account of three modes of self-transcendence. Although no explicit and pre-ordained end point is to be commonly attained, there is an implicit *telos* in the sense that the very process of self-transcendence is understood to be naturally ordered intellectually, morally, and religiously. Wartofsky, following Pittendrigh, suggests that this type of development is "teleonomic" rather than "teleological" since it is not a process of conscious goal-seeking with an explicit end in view.[17] Furthermore, Lonergan suggests that a person may experience all three types of conversion. Here, the key factor is the principle of sublation. To be sublated literally means to be carried under or to be carried along. A lower function in process is drawn into configuration of a higher process without losing the lower. Accordingly, what is eventuated in each type of conversion is integrated into the self and carried forward to a deeper and fuller realization of the self. Sublation then is essentially a principle of coherence at work in the process of self-transcendence. Through sublation, intellectual conversion goes beyond mere facts to meaning and moral conversion goes beyond the pursuit of truth to *praxis*, i.e., the practice of values as ends in themselves. Similarly, religious conversion is the enacted narrative of a life that is totally given over in love to the Transcendent. This relationship is the ultimate basis of all meaning and value. It is the *telos* of self-transcendence.

By now it should be clear that our structuralist typologies of conversion lack an understanding of self-transcendence. Earlier I investigated conversion as though it were simply an organic process with no ontic dimensions. Similarly, Fowler's many options for a stadial-developmental view of conversion are also grounded in the content/structure distinction. Granted this distinction is necessary, given the epistemological foundations of faith development theory, but it is not sufficient. We must also be attentive to the structure/function distinction. The latter is our point of *rapprochement* between faith development theory and conversion.

Lonergan's use of the concept of sublation is a good example of what I mean by function. Lonergan is not concerned with an analysis of sequentially ordered stages of intellectual, moral, and religious conversion. Nor is he concerned with organismic processes governing sublation. Rather, he addresses the issue of how these two dynamic processes result in a more coherent experience of self-transcendence. In this sense his interpretation of conversion is as pragmatic as that of William James. In sum, while it may be helpful to offer a structural-developmental typology in conversion, we should bear in mind the fact that the adult stages of faith do not indicate an increasing approximation to ultimate faith. If this were the case, Fowler would have had to begin with a definition of ultimate faith and then demonstrate how it is approximated at each stage. Instead, Fowler concentrates on the psychological development of faith. Nevertheless, the issue of ultimate faith cannot be easily laid aside. It haunts us, particularly when faith development is misconstrued as a "hothouse" for accelerating the production of faith. The principle of sublation helps us to avoid such a crass interpretation of faith by affirming faith development as an open process of maturation. Consequently, stage six should be viewed not as a final stage of a closed system but as the outcome of religious conversion and the sublation of stage five. Obviously, this radically challenges the Piagetian structuralist orientation of Fowler's theory—not stages one through four which may be correlated empirically with Piaget's stages, but stages five and six, the stages of adult faith.

I suggest that conversion is necessary to move to stages five and six. Moreover, it seems to me that the function of "dialectical thinking"—structural advancement beyond formal operational thinking—could be explained in terms of the sublation of intellectual, moral, and religious conversions within a single consciousness. The tensional and paradoxical character of stage five may very well be indicative of the sublation of rational, moral, and religious conversions; hence the open-endedness of meaning-making and the dialogical character of stage five. Stage five sublates the intellectual biases of stage four and affirms a pluralistic view of truth. Stage five sublates the moralism of stage four and affirms a multi-perspectival pursuit of all values.

And, most importantly, what is taken to be "intuitions of universality" that are perhaps the source of the ability to hold together its polarities and conflicts may well be indications of religious conversion.

At stage six, the notion of sublation is even more critical. At this time there is no structural-empirical evidence to support the existence of this stage. Consequently, Fowler relies on the religious classics of the Christian and other traditions for images of the *eschaton*. He finds it necessary to affirm the open-endedness of the faith stages by invoking the traditional symbolizations of what is to be expected beyond the fulfillment of meaning-making in the here and now. In so doing, not only has he arrived at the universal through the particular, but he has moved away from the content/structure problem and has become more attentive to the practice of faith in the transformation and conversion of our lives as we become mature mediators of the Kingdom of God. Such faith is confirmed and reconfirmed by our participation in an intensified journey into the classic rites and symbols of our particular tradition. Herein lies the significance of the Rite of Christian Initiation of Adults.

Faith Development and the RCIA

The various canonico-liturgical documents of the catechumenate are religious classics of the Christian tradition. The Rite of Christian Initiation of Adults (RCIA) is predicated upon the imperative that we enter into conversation liturgically with these classic rites and symbols. Each stage of the RCIA reflects a progressive integration and intensification of the catechumen's relationship to God, Church, and the World.

As far as faith development theory is concerned, it makes sense to begin with the adult form of stage three, synthetic-conventional faith. The aspects of a faith stage relevant to the RCIA are social perspective-taking, bounds of social awareness, form of world coherence, and symbolic functioning. Stage three is identified mainly by the synthesis of conventional ideas and attitudes of significant others. Its world-view (*Weltanschauung*) is tacit and is mediated through interpersonal relationships. Authority is vested in persons on the basis of their manifest virtues, for example, honesty, and the conventional roles played in the maintenance of community. The RCIA is grounded in sacraments that stress the candidate's participation in a covenantal community, namely, baptism, confirmation, and the Eucharist. It is reasonable therefore to expect that the Church community at stage three would view the RCIA primarily in terms of its function in preserving traditional homogeneous values and meanings. Rituals and symbols would be perceived as instrumental to the maintenance of interpersonal relationships and valued on the basis of their ability to evoke feelings of belonging and continuity with the tradition. At stage three symbols and rituals are not demythologized. On the contrary, their interpretation is effected by trusted authorities. These relationships and the charisma generated in the liturgy are the matrix of the convert's identification with the community of faith. At stage three the mentor relationship is very important. The problem before us is how to explain the maturation of faith beyond stage three. Do we simply move to stage four?

The problem with stage four is that it reflects the strong individualism characteristic of American culture, and the rationalism characteristic of Piagetian neo-Kantianism. The critical distancing of the self from the matrix of conventional relationships stands in sharp contrast to the RCIA's mandate for a deepening of the neophyte's identification with the faith community. We may well ask, therefore, whether the RCIA is untenable to a person in stage four. In terms of the content/structure dynamism, the ideational and symbolic content of the RCIA could be structurally assimilated and accommodated at stage four, but would assume a distinctive rational critical form. The RCIA would be viewed as a system that is conceptually mediated, ordered by rules, and rationally defended. But would such a posture be faithful to the spirit and intent of the RCIA?

Let me reiterate my earlier suggestion that Fowler's structural-developmental interpretation of faith needs to be supplemented by a theory of self-transcendence. Psychologically, this necessitates the formulation of a theory of the construction of the self throughout the life cycle. One such theory is offered by

Kegan who concentrates on the self's meaning-making activity.[18] This theory, however, is rooted firmly in Piagetian structuralism and does not address the self's relation to the transcendent. Erikson, on the other hand, is more sensitive to the fact that identity is shaped not only by the interaction of self and world, but also by a consciousness of the self's relation to the Other—the ground of being itself. Hence he underscores the importance of religion in the shaping of faith from early in childhood, particularly as it ritualizes the presence of the "numinous" in identity formation.

> The numinous assures us, ever again, of *separateness transcended* and yet also of *distinctiveness confirmed,* and thus of the very basis of a sense of "I." Religion and art are the institutions with the strongest traditional claim on the cultivation of numinosity, as can be discerned in the details of rituals by which the numinous is shared with a congregation of other "I's"—all now sharing one all-embracing "I Am" (Jehovah).[19]

In addition, Erikson's final stage of integrity not only reaffirms the ontic character of identity formation, but also the fact that the shaping of the whole person ultimately is a religious process.

Now we can focus more closely on transition from stage three. What we discern as an ideological propensity in stage four may be a need by persons to objectify the self's relation to the transcendent. Kegan argues that what functions as the *internal* point of reference for the self at one stage becomes an *external* point of reference in the next stage. For example, at stage three "objective truth" is subordinated to the interpersonal relationships from which the self derives its meaning. This is reversed at stage four where objective truth is now the reference point of the community of faith. Were Fowler to draw more on Erikson, one possible outcome would be a greater integration of the numinous into the self. This is particularly evident at stage four where the mystery of the self's relation to the transcendent (*participation mystique*) is filtered through the lenses of rational critical consciousness. Lost is the sense of "a *primal other*—the I's counterpart."[20] Instead we see a self that is striving to preserve some semblance of autonomy. As a result, ritualization is reduced to a form of "private ritualism" that is symptomatic of a culture in which individualism ("the self-made man") and tribalism are among its primary virtues.

Somehow the catechumenate must uphold psychological principles, theological tenets, and ethical values that counteract the negative elements in stage four. This I see as the most significant contribution of the RCIA to faith development theory. Stage four's reticence for the ambiguous needs to be balanced by an affection for the ultimate mystery of faith—the *mysterium tremendum et fascinans*. This experience, notes Erikson, "like the best things in life, cannot be contrived."[21]

Stage five poses a different set of problems for the RCIA. Persons in this stage are able to maintain a coherent sense of self while participating in a pluralistic world in which truth is apprehended through many different traditions. Symbols are understood as multivalent and paradoxical.

The salient issue for the RCIA is the recovery of tradition—recovering the redemptive power of the biblical narrative and the universal salvific meaning of the sacraments of baptism, confirmation, and the Eucharist. At stage five a central concern is the discernment of the universal in the particular. But discerning the universal necessitates a journey of intensification into the liturgy and creeds of one's particular faith community. In other words, the RCIA is just as important to the person at stage five as it is to the person at stages two or three. The main difference is that the person at stage five would be particularly attentive to the ways in which the RCIA nurtures a level of consciousness of the sacraments that holds together the liturgical expressions of a particular faith community and the intuitions of universality disclosed in its symbols. Catechumens in the earlier stages might find stage five's pluralistic consciousness and openness to the truths disclosed in other religious traditions rather unsettling. For such persons the spiritual intentionality of the RCIA is limited to its ability to immerse the catechumen in powerful relationships with a spiritual director or mentor. This is characteristic of stage three. At stage four a primary concern would be the certainty and ideological purity of the beliefs held by the RCIA. In contrast, the critical issue at stage five is what is meant by conversion to the Church universal. What does it mean to be participating in the rites of a particular tradition, a particular faith community, while being radically transformed by the trans-historical, trans-cultural, and eternal power of God's love? For Christians, stage five holds us firmly grounded in the tradition but provokes our consciousness of the tradition's inescapable demand that ultimately the self must surrender even the tradition itself and empty itself in God. This is the meaning of *kenosis* which presumes religious conversion.

In conclusion, the *telos* of the RCIA demands a level of spirituality that is not simply attained by stage transition. Stage change is simply a metaphor for the breakdown of coherent meaning and value. It requires *metanoia*—intellectual, moral, and religious. While the support of a community of the faithful is necessary for faith development, intellectual conversion is also necessary for the catechumen to be transformed by the numinousness of the Rite. Here the spiritual director must guard against idolism, particularly in its vulgar form of carbonated charisma. Moral conversion is necessary to grasp what Erikson calls the "*judicious* principle of ritualization." Here "the law" and "the word" are combined. A readiness to accept the spirit of the word that conveys lawfulness is an integral aspect of this development. But such judiciousness could be undermined by *legalism*. In addition, for Erikson, the most serious threat to the *dramatic* element in ritualization is *moralism*. These types of responses to ritualization are established early in childhood and are the antecedents of later ways of responding to the "totally Other" in adulthood.

Both Erikson and Fowler leave us at the threshold of religious conversion. Their respective stage theories are disturbing reminders of a more profound spiritual hunger for transcendence beyond the here and now. If stage four is a necessary nodal point in the journey of faith before we can enter into a level of apprehending the paradoxes of faith, then it is important to assess the effectiveness of religious institutions in providing alternative images and symbols to counteract territorial defensiveness and "pseudospeciation" of stage four. The RCIA has such potential. Not only does it recapitulate the transforming power inherent in the rites of the Christian tradition, it also reaffirms the public character of the Church. Baptism, confirmation, and the Eucharist are powerful events in the intensive journey into the universality of God through a particular tradition. This is what stage five describes. However, this description needs to be supplemented by a view of religious conversion as the ultimate transformation of the self through faith. Lonergan's view of religious conversion as a falling in love with God not only adds to developmental stages a notion of sublation but, more importantly, reaffirms St. Paul's conviction that integral to the development of faith is the development of love and hope for an age to come.

Notes

1. James Fowler and Sam Keen, *Life Maps: Conversations on the Journey of Faith*, Minnesota: Winston Press, 1978; James Fowler, *Stages of Faith: The Psychology of Human Development and the Quest for Meaning*, San Francisco: Harper & Row, 1981.

2. Jean Piaget, *Structuralism*, trans. C. Maschler, New York: Basic Books, 1970.

3. Erik Erikson, *Childhood and Society*, New York: Norton, 1950.

4. Wilfred Cantwell Smith, *Faith and Belief*, New Jersey: Princeton, 1979.

5. David Tracy, *The Analogical Imagination*, New York: Crossroad, 1981.

6. A. Mayeaux, "The Moral Life as Narrative Quest." Unpublished manuscript.

7. Tracy, 371.

8. D. Elkind, "The Child's Conception of His Religious Denomination I: The Jewish Child," *Journal of Genetic Psychology* 99 (1961) 209–215; "The Child's Conception of His Religious Denomination II: The Catholic Child," *Journal of Genetic Psychology*

101 (1962) 185–193; "The Child's Conception of His Religious Denomination III: The Protestant Child," *Journal of Genetic Psychology* 103 (1963) 291–304.

9. R. Goldman, *Religious Thinking from Childhood to Adolescence*, London: Routledge & Kegan Paul, 1964; *Readiness for Religion*, New York: Seabury, 1965.

10. K. Riegel, "Dialectic Operations: The Final Period of Cognitive Development," *Human Development* 16 (1973) 346–370.

11. M. Basseches, "Beyond Closed-System Problem Solving: A Study of Meta-Systematic Aspects of Mature Thought." Unpublished Ph.D. Dissertation, Harvard University, 1978.

12. Jane Loevinger, *Ego Development*, San Francisco: Jossey-Bass, 1976.

13. Erikson, *The Life Cycle Completed*, 9.

14. Romney Moseley, "Religious Conversion: A Structural-Developmental Analysis," Ph.D. Dissertation, Harvard University, 1978.

15. Fowler, *Stages of Faith*, 285.

16. Bernard Lonergan, "Theology in Its New Context and the Dimensions of Conversion," in Walter Conn (ed.), *Conversion: Perspectives on Personal and Social Transformation*, New York: Society of St. Paul, 1978, 3–21.

17. M. Wartofsky, "From Praxis to Logos: Genetic Psychology and Physics," in T. Mischel (ed.), *Cognitive Development and Epistemology*, New York: Academic Press, 1971.

18. R. Kegan, *The Evolving Self*, Cambridge: Harvard University Press, 1982.

19. Erikson, *The Life Cycle Completed*, 45.

20. *Ibid.*, 44.

21. *Ibid.*

Notes on Contributors

Rev. Edward K. Braxton—A priest of the Archdiocese of Chicago, Father Braxton is director of the Catholic Student Center at the University of Chicago. His many publications include *The Wisdom Community*, and he has spoken widely in this country and abroad. Father Braxton has taught at Harvard University, Notre Dame, and the Catholic University of America.

Rev. Louis John Cameli—Born in Chicago, Father Cameli earned his STL degree from the Gregorian University, Rome, in 1970 and his STD degree, with a specialization in spirituality, in 1975. He is currently associate professor of spirituality and director of spiritual life at St. Mary of the Lake Seminary, Mundelein, Ill.

Michael Brennan Dick, M.A., S.T.L., Ph.D.—Dr. Dick received his degree in theology from the Gregorian University in Rome; he pursued work in biblical studies at the Biblicum in Rome and at The Johns Hopkins University where he received his doctorate in Semitic Languages. He is assistant professor in Religious Studies at Siena College in Loudonville, N.Y. Dr. Dick has taught at Dickinson College and Bennington College prior to Siena. He has published in *Catholic Biblical Quarterly*, *Vetus Testamentum*, and *Zeitschrift für alttestamentliche Wissenschaft*.

Rev. Regis A. Duffy, O.F.M.—Father Duffy is professor of theology at The Washington Theological Union and has been Visiting Professor at Princeton Theological Seminary and the University of Notre Dame. He has authored *Real Presence* and *A Roman Catholic Theology of Pastoral Care.*

Rev. Robert D. Duggan—Father Duggan is a priest of the Archdiocese of Washington D.C. His doctoral dissertation from the Catholic University of America was a study of conversion in the Rite of Christian Initiation of Adults, and he has written and spoken extensively on this subject. Father Duggan is currently assigned to Holy Cross Parish, Garrett Park, Maryland and is a part-time lecturer at the Washington Theological Union.

Rev. James B. Dunning—Father Dunning is presently coordinator of the North American Forum on the Catechumenate; he was formerly president and executive director of National Organization for the Continuing Education of Roman Catholic Clergy, and coordinator of Adult Education and Continuing Education for Priests for the Archdiocese of Seattle. He is the author of *New Wine: New Wineskins* and *Ministries: Sharing God's Gifts.*

Rev. Romney M. Moseley—Born in Barbados, West Indies, ordained in the Anglican Church, Father Moseley graduated from Boston University and received the B.D. and Ph.D. from Harvard University. He is presently Assistant Professor of Theology and Human Development, Candler School of Theology, Emory University.

Mark Searle—Mark Searle was born in England in 1941 and subsequently studied in Europe, obtaining a doctorate in liturgical studies under Balthasar Fischer in Trier, Germany. He is currently Associate Professor of Theology at the University of Notre Dame and director of the Graduate Program in Liturgical Studies. He is past president of the North American Academy of Liturgy and the author of *Christening, Liturgy Made Simple,* and other writings.